Sankey Goldschmith

Goldsmith's Traveller

With introduction, life of the author, argument, and notes. Second Canadian

Edition

Sankey Goldschmith

Goldsmith's Traveller

With introduction, life of the author, argument, and notes. Second Canadian Edition

ISBN/EAN: 9783337212315

Printed in Europe, USA, Canada, Australia, Japan

Cover: Foto ©Andreas Hilbeck / pixelio.de

More available books at **www.hansebooks.com**

CANADA SCHOOL JOURNAL.

Recommended by the Minister of Education in Ontario.
Recommended by the Board of Education for Quebec.
Recommended by the Supt. of Education, New Brunswick.

"An excellent publication."—*Pacific School Journal, Sanfrancisco.*

"The Canada School Journal, published by Adam Miller & Co., Toronto. is a live educational journal, and should be in the hands of every teacher." —*Stratford Weekly Herald.*

I cordially recommend the "Canada School Journal" to the teachers of New Brunswick.

THEODORE H. RAND, Chief Supt. Education.

EDITORIAL COMMITTEE.

J. A. McLellan, M.A., LL.D., High School Inspector.
Thomas Kirkland, M.A., Science Master, Normal School.
James Hughes, Public School Inspector, Toronto.
Alfred Baker, B.A., Math. Tutor. University College, Toronto

PROVINCIAL EDITORS.

Ontario—J. M. Buchan, M.A., High School Inspector.
G. W. Ross, M.P., Public School Inspector.
J. C. Glashan, Public School Inspector.
Quebec—W. Dale, M.A., Rector High School.
S. P. Robins, M.A., Supt. Protestant School, Montreal.
New Brunswick—J. Bennett, Ph.D., Supt. City School, Montreal.
Nova Scotia—T. C. Sunmichrast, Registrar, University of Halifax.
Manitoba—John Cameron, B.A., Winnipeg.
British Columbia—John Jessop, Supt. of Education.

CONTRIBUTORS.

Rev. E. Ryerson, D.D., LL.D., late Chief Supt. of Education.
J. G. Hodgins, LL.D., Deputy Minister of Education.
Theodore Rand, A.M., D.C.L., Supt. Education, New Brunswick.
W. Crocket, A.M., Principal Normal School, Fredericton, N.B.
J. B. Calkin, M.A., Principal Normal School, Truro, N.S.
Dr. Bayne, Halifax High School.
Robert Potts, M.A., Cambridge, Eng.
Daniel Wilson, LL.D., Prof. of History and Eng. Lit., Univ. Coll., Toronto
Rev. S. S. Nelles, D.D., LL.D., Pres. University Victoria College.
Rev. H. G. Maddock, M.A., F.G.S., Fellow of Clare College, Cambridge, Professor of Classics, Trinity College, Toronto.
M. McVicar, Ph.D., LL.D., Principal State Normal and Training School, Potsdam, N. Y.
Rev. A. F. Kemp, LL.D., Principal Brantford Young Ladies' College
Geo. Dickson, B.A., Collegiate Institute, Hamilton.
Prof. John A. Macoun, Albert College, Belleville.
Rev. Prof. G. M. Meacham, M.A., Numadza, Japan.
Wm. Johnson, M.A., Principal Agricultural College, Guelph.
John C. McCabe, M.A., Principal Normal School, Ottawa.
Dr. S. P. May, Secretary Centennial Education Committee.
Prof. J. E. Wells, Canadian Literary Institute, Woodstock.
Rev. J. J. Hare, B.A., Ontario Ladies' College, Whitby.
James Carlyle, M.D., Math. Master Normal School, Toronto
Geo. Baptic, M.D., Science Master Normal School, Ottawa.
R. Lewis, Teacher of Elocution, Toronto.
Prof. R. Bawson, Belleville.
J. J. Tilley, Inspector Public Schools, Durham.

CANADA SCHOOL JOURNAL

Is issued 1st of each month from the Office of Publication, 11 Wellington Street West, Toronto.
Subscription $1 per year, payable in advance.

ADAM MILLER & CO.,
Publishers, Toronto.

Miller & Co.'s English School Classics.

GOLDSMITH'S TRAVELLER:

WITH INTRODUCTION, LIFE OF THE AUTHOR, ARGUMENT, AND NOTES.

BY

C. SANKEY, M.A.,

ASSISTANT-MASTER AT MARLBOROUGH COLLEGE.

SECOND CANADIAN COPYRIGHT EDITION.

TORONTO:

ADAM MILLER & CO.

1879.

Entered according to Act of Parliament of Canada, in the Office of the Minister of Agriculture, by ADAM MILLER & Co., in the year 1879.

LIFE AND INTRODUCTION.

OLIVER GOLDSMITH, like Swift and Steele in the preceding generation, Edmund Burke among his contemporaries, and R. B. Sheridan among his successors, was an Irishman; for his family, though of Saxon extraction, had been for some generations settled in Ireland. He was born on November 29, 1728, in an unpretending parsonage at Pallas, an out-of-the-way and almost inaccessible hamlet in the county of Longford. His father, Charles Goldsmith, was a clergyman of the then Established Church; his mother, Anne, was daughter of the Rev. Oliver Jones, master of the Diocesan School at Elphin. Oliver Goldsmith was the second son in a family consisting of four sons and two daughters. Of his strong family affection we have ample proofs. Seldom has a son left a picture of a father drawn with such fond fidelity as that of the village preacher in the *Deserted Village;* and his correspondence shows how warmly he was attached to his brothers, and especially to his eldest brother, Henry, to whom *The Traveller* is dedicated.

When Oliver was two years old, his father was made rector of Lissoy, or Lishoy, in Westmeath; here the young poet's education began at the hands of a maid-servant, Elizabeth Delap, by whom he was taught his letters, and pronounced "impenetrably stupid." In his seventh year he was promoted to the village school; for the limited income of his father, already strained to the utmost in providing for the education of his eldest son, could ill bear any increased expenditure: his new instructor—one Thomas Byrne, of aboriginal Irish descent, an enthusiastic admirer and, in his own way, an imitator of the ancient Irish bards—had been quarter-master in the army, and had seen service in the war of the Succession in Spain; and he probably formed the mind of his young pupil more by wonderful legends of banshees and rapparees, and no less marvellous narratives of his own adventures, than by direct instruction in the rudiments of learning. Yet the boy, even at eight years, shewed precocious signs of poetical genius—"he lisped in numbers, for the numbers came."

It had been originally determined that Oliver should be put to a trade when comparatively young, for the small income and large family of his father seemed to make it impossible for him to receive as thorough an education as his elder brother; but soon after this time the entreaties of his mother produced a change in the family plans, and Oliver was removed from the village school, first to Elphin, then to Athlone, and lastly to Edgeworthstown, that he might be prepared for the University. As a school-boy he was quick and clever, though certainly not too industrious; but he gave sufficient promise of future excellence to induce some wealthy friends and kinsmen—among whom may be mentioned especially the Rev. Thomas Contarine—to contribute largely to the expenses of his education.

On June 11, 1744, he was admitted as a sizar to Trinity College, Dublin; but his career was not to be as successful as his friends had fondly hoped. The tutor under whom he was placed was harsh, violent, and unsympathetic; the pupil was thoughtless, eccentric, and irregular: he neglected his legitimate studies to write street-ballads, which he sold for five shillings apiece, and then broke the college-rules by stealing out of gates at

) What poet imitated Goldsmith and in what poems? Crabbe and in how far was he succes- in his [fr] imitation

) What is the nominal object of "The Traveller"

Is the object attained.

The nominal object of "The Traveller is to show that the happiness of the individual does not depend upon the form of Government

the principal happiness to the sensual bliss will Italia is with swiss is patriotic with French is Gayety with Britain Liberty

and all are capable of being
carried into ~~sweeter~~ effect
~~the nominal effect~~
~~The poet imitated~~
The poems of Crabby were
The Village & The Parish
Register
—————————————

(1) Tell what you know of the person
to whom the poem is dedicated
Westmeath was where Henry
preached
—————————————

Give in your own language
the substance of Goldsmith
reasoning about the inhabitants
of barren states; and examine
the correctness of his conclu-

night to hear them sung. On one occasion, to celebrate his success in gaining an exhibition of the value of thirty shillings, he gave a dance in his attics to some gay friends in the city. Hence we find him, after receiving some perhaps unnecessarily stern chastisement from his tutor, selling books and clothes, intending to embark at Cork to try his luck in foreign parts; but spending his last shilling in Dublin, and finally, through his brother's intercession, sullenly consenting to a reconciliation with his tutor, and returning to college. Indolent, though occasionally brilliant, he did not graduate till 1749; and then followed two years of idleness, vagrancy, and thoughtlessness. No profession could be found for which he was fitted; the church and the bar were both attempted, but without success—a pair of scarlet breeches is said to have excluded him from the one, and an imprudent fit of gambling from the other—and his perpetual escapades and adventures must have seriously embarrassed his widowed mother, and tried to the utmost the long-suffering affection of that paragon of uncles, good Mr. Contarine.

At the end of the year 1752, Goldsmith was sent to Edinburgh to study medicine, but 'caelum non animum mutant qui trans mare currunt;' and his Scotch career was characterized by the same heedlessness, good nature, and desultoriness which had marked all his previous life. Though his attendance in the class-rooms of the professors had been by no means regular—for he had tried a tutorship with the Duke of Hamilton, travelled on pony-back in the Highlands, and gambled and sung his hours away—in a year or two's time he thought himself sufficiently advanced in medical science to ask for his uncle's consent to a sojourn at Leyden to complete his studies. Thither accordingly he set out, embarking in a Scotch ship bound for Bordeaux, choosing a somewhat circuitous route to his journey's end. But by a fortunate mistake Goldsmith, with some others of the ship's company, was detained in gaol at Newcastle, while the ship proceeded on her voyage, and was lost with all hands at the mouth of the Garonne; and Goldsmith reached Leyden, *viâ* Rotterdam. Here he resided about a year, devoting some of his time and energy to the lectures of the medical professors, and more to the pleasures of the gaming-table. Then he determined to leave Holland for the purpose of extending his foreign travels; but of the money lent to him for that object, he squandered the greater part in play, spent all the rest in a present of the rarest and most costly flower-roots for his uncle in Ireland, and started on his European tour a penniless pedestrian, with one clean shirt and his flute; but with a good constitution, a light heart, and abundance of animal spirits.

An extract from *The Vicar of Wakefield*, put into the mouth of the wanderer, George Primrose, is said to furnish a tolerably accurate account of Goldsmith's ordinary mode of providing the necessaries of life during his travels: " I had some knowledge of music, with a tolerable voice, and now turned what was my amusement into a present means of subsistence. I passed among the harmless peasants of Flanders, and among such of the French as were poor enough to be very merry, for I ever found them sprightly in proportion to their wants. Whenever I approached a peasant's house towards nightfall I played one of my most merry tunes, and that procured me not only a lodging, but subsistence for the next day. . . . . In all the foreign universities and convents there are upon certain days philosophical theses maintained against every adventitious disputant, for which, if the champion opposes with any dexterity, he can claim a gratuity in money, a dinner, and a bed for one night. In this manner therefore I fought my way towards England, walked along from city to city, examined mankind more nearly, and, if

9 To what class of poetry does the Traveller belong? Didactic. Name other poems of this class? Essay on Man. Night Thoughts. Cowpers task. Parish Register. The Village. Pleasures of imagination.

) Quote the Thesis which Goldsm sets out to ~~prose~~ prove (lines 75—80)

Contrast according to Goldsmith the Blessings of Nature and art of Classical Didactic poems Virgils Georgics

The Most famous descriptive in English language is Thompson's Seasons

10 How far is the description of Italy correct
How far was his delineation of the character of the inhabitants ~~first~~ when he wrote. How far

7. Know ——
of Italy and Italians. —

Point out any particulars
in which Goldsmith has
unjustly censured the French
and make what addition
seem necessary to a complete
description of the French character

They are very fond of war?
"   "   " " " ingenious?
"   "   " " " hopeful?

Quote some of the happier expressions
used in the description of Holland

In poorer of the English, were
too independent independent
Outlawed but the Dutch
became servants for the richer

I may so express it, saw both sides of the picture." He travelled through Flanders, parts of France and Germany, through Switzerland and the north of Italy, taking an uncongenial tutorship at Geneva, and abandoning it at Marseilles, staying for six months and perhaps graduating in medicine at Padua, visiting Verona, Florence, and Venice ; and finally, after the death of his good uncle, who had probably contributed in part to his maintenance, landing at Dover in 1756.

The poet arrived in London, as he himself says, "without friends, recommendation, money, or impudence." His plain face, shabby dress, Irish brogue, and eccentric antecedents, made it difficult for him to get employment. He first became an assistant master in a school, but it is uncertain how long his flighty genius endured the irksome monotony of such an occupation. He is next found helping in a chemist's laboratory near Fish Street Hill ; and soon after, through the kind assistance of Dr. Sleigh, an old Edinburgh fellow-student, he set up as an independent physician, at first at Bankside, Southwark, and afterwards in the Temple. But his medical skill was but small ; the fact of his degree in medicine is very doubtful ; the only patient whom we know that he doctored, he killed, and that was himself; and Beauclerk's witticism is well known ; "I do not practise," said Goldsmith ; " I make it a rule to prescribe only for my friends." "Pray, dear doctor," was the reply, "alter your rule, and prescribe only for your enemies." His patients, by his own account, were numerous, but unremunerative, and he began to practise literature as a second string to his bow. Thus he became a literary hack, or, in his own words, "a regular Swiss in the service of the booksellers ;" and so "with very little practice as a physician, and very little reputation as a poet, he made a shift to live."

But though Goldsmith had now touched the outer

circles of the literary world, no one seems at present to have guessed the genius of the young *littérateur*, nor was he himself conscious that poetry and literary composition was to be henceforth his main employment. Indeed for some time he returned to the profession which he had found so disagreeable, and became, for £20 a year, superintendent of a school at Peckham; and in 1758 he was appointed physician to a factory in India. The chief obstacle that prevented him from at once setting sail to amass untold wealth in the East, on a salary of £100 a year, was that he had not money enough to pay for his outfit and passage. He had previously published works of minor importance—a "catch-penny" *Life of Voltaire*, completed in four weeks, for twenty pounds; and *The Memoirs of a Protestant condemned to the Gallies of France for his Religion*, for which he received the same sum—but now he was to venture something greater. Accordingly all his friends in England and Ireland were importuned to circulate proposals for the publication by subscription of an *Enquiry into the Present State of Polite Literature in Europe*. This work did more for its author than raise a sum sufficient for his Indian outfit; it raised his value in the eyes of the booksellers, and as their patronage increased, his visions of Oriental riches waned. He published *The Bee*, contributed criticisms to various reviews and newspapers, wrote regularly for the *Monthly Review* for half a year, was regularly retained by Newbery, the publisher, at a salary of £100 a year, made the acquaintance of Smollett and other literary friends, and advanced from squalid and ill-, or almost un-furnished, lodgings in Green Arbour Court, Old Bailey, to a more respectable habitation in Wine-office Court, Fleet Street. During his residence here he first met Dr. Johnson, who was then the king, not to say the tyrant, of the literary world. About twenty years older than Gold-

Change took pla
ce of Goldsmith
introducing p
ublic, they Ind
author itself
Relative of trad
ce way, the disc
ruca + Civil
mpetitie vication
ey of a sea ror

ment by asse
s the Port dys
val & Production
Island

the reasoning ris
so exclusive
lines which conta
to the ports per

9) What were the causes of the decline of the Italian commerce in Italy

(14) Whence was alliteration introduced into modern English from old English

Point out the finer touches in the delineation of the French character

Give the description of the peasantry in the different countries described

Macaulay

smith, he had himself known what it was to fight his way through difficulty and disappointment to eminence and fame in the world of letters. The fortitude with which he had borne his troubles had not hardened his heart, nor was his real nature less warm and sympathetic because his manners were *brusque* and his exterior rough. With these two acquaintance soon ripened into friendship, and friendship became intimacy. Here also Goldsmith wrote *The Vicar of Wakefield;* but no sooner was this work finished than his landlady arrested him for arrears of debt. Goldsmith, in extremities, sent off to Johnson, who came at once, and took the manuscript to Newbery, to whom he sold it for sixty pounds, and thus obtained the freedom of his friend. The book, however, was not published for two or three years, not indeed till Goldsmith had gained reputation by the publication of *The Traveller*, which was even at that moment lying finished in his desk.

During the years 1762, 1763, and 1764 he was engaged in literary work of a miscellaneous character: history, biography, criticism, essay-writing, occupied him in turn. His works include a *Life of Beau Nash*, an *Art of Poetry*, *Letters on English History*, and especially a series of letters reprinted from *The Ledger*, and republished under the title of *The Citizen of the World*. He was also gradually advancing, in spite of much recklessness and imprudence, to an important position in the literary society of the time. His friends were now more numerous and influential, and his first-floor apartments at No. 2, Brick Court, in the Temple, were furnished in a manner suitable to the distinguished society whom he used to entertain there. In 1764 began the meetings of that celebrated Literary Club, which the pages of Boswell have rendered so familiar. It was originally proposed by Sir Joshua Reynolds to Johnson and Burke, and Goldsmith was at once admitted as one of the original nine who met for supper and conversation on Fridays at the Turk's Head, in Gerard Street, Soho.

In 1765 *The Traveller* was published. Part of it had been written by him during his travels in Switzerland; but the poem had arrived very slowly at completion. For two years or more, encouraged by the approval of Dr. Johnson, it had been the delight of Goldsmith's few leisure hours to polish and prune this his masterpiece. The effect produced by its publication was soon visible: four editions were required within eight months, and Goldsmith rose from the position of a comparatively obscure essayist to that of the first poet of the age. Very soon after this *The Vicar of Wakefield* appeared; and the ballad of *The Hermit*, which is inserted in the novel, and also was printed separately, confirmed the author's reputation as a poet.

But Goldsmith was now to show the wide range of his powers by distinguishing himself in an entirely fresh branch of literature. In January, 1768, his comedy, *The Good-natured Man*, was produced for the first time, under George Colman the elder, at Covent Garden. It had been written some little time before, and was originally offered to Garrick for representation at Drury Lane; but after much hesitation, in spite of the strong recommendation of Johnson and Burke, it was rejected. Nor indeed, though it obtained £500 for its author, and was introduced to the public by a prologue written by Johnson, did it prove a great success. Cumberland, Kelly, and the sentimental comedy were victorious, and after a short run of nine or ten nights it was withdrawn, and Goldsmith was not heard of again as a theatrical author for five years.

The Deserted Village appeared in May, 1770. It is said that Goldsmith was four or five years collecting the materials for this poem, and that the actual composition

What would you infer as to Goldsmith's appreciation of the sublime in nature of the Swiss scenery.

What peculiarity of the poetry of the eighteenth century are seen in 273 & 280? Personification

Characterize Goldsmith's description of the climate, scenery & inhabitants of Britain

Point out the particulars
in which Goldsmith is unjust
to the Dutch? Cowardice
What ills are represented as
rising in England from freedom

extended over more than two years. This is very probable; for we know that it was only during the intervals of prose composition that he could apply himself to this labour of love. It was to his prose writings that he had to look for his daily bread. "Pay no regard to the muses" —such is his advice to a friend—"I have always found productions in prose more sought after and better paid for. . . . . By courting the muses I shall starve ; but by my other labours I shall eat, drink, have good clothes, and enjoy the luxuries of life." He wrote popular histories—a *History of England*, for five hundred pounds; a *Roman History*, and an abridgment of the *Roman History*, *Lives of Parnell and Bolingbroke*, besides introductions and prefaces to books by other authors. But these works, though highly praised by Dr. Johnson and other contemporary critics, were not of any great permanent value. Goldsmith had not the painstaking conscientiousness in the investigation of details which alone can make a man a great historian; nor does he take a much higher rank as a biographer. Still, in all his writings he shows that easy and fascinating style which Johnson said would make a Natural History by him as entertaining as a Persian tale.

However, the reputation of Goldsmith as an historian must have been very considerable; for on the establishment of the Royal Academy of Painting, in 1768, the honorary office of Professor of Ancient History was conferred on Goldsmith. In a letter to his brother Maurice, dated January, 1770, he alludes to his new appointment: "The king has lately been pleased to make me Professor of Ancient History in a Royal Academy of Painting which he has just established; but there is no salary annexed, and I took it rather as a compliment to the institution than any benefit to myself. Honours to one in my situation are something like ruffles to one that wants a shirt." After Goldsmith's death the professorship was given to Gibbon, who was succeeded in his turn by Mitford, the historian of Greece.

After a short visit to Paris with two ladies, named Horneck, during the summer of 1770, Goldsmith retired to the solitude of a farm-house, near the sixth mile-stone on the Edgware Road, where he was far enough from London smoke and noise to enjoy the refreshing air of the country, and yet near enough to partake sufficiently freely of London life and London pleasures. Here he occupied himself partly with a new comedy, partly with his *Natural History*. On September 7th, 1771, he writes to Bennet Langton, Esq. : "The *Natural History* is about half finished, and I will shortly finish the rest. God knows, I am tired of this kind of finishing, which is but bungling work, and that not so much my fault as the fault of my scurvy circumstances." However, *The History of the Earth* and of *Animated Nature* did not appear till 1774. For this extensive work, in eight vols. 8vo., the author received from his publisher £850. He was not a naturalist any more than an historian; as deficient in powers of scientific observation as in taste for historical research; his facts were obtained secondhand,* and the most grotesque travellers' tales are told with a charming innocence and credulity; but the book is as good as wide, though desultory reading, dignified reflections, and a graceful style can make it. The comedy, which he was writing at the same time, had appeared previously. After rejecting the title, *The Old House a New Inn*, Goldsmith resolved to call it, *The Mistakes of a Night; or, She Stoops to Conquer*. It was first acted in March, 1773, under George Colman, sen., at Covent Garden. It was dedicated to Dr. Johnson ; and the author writes

* *Ex. gra.* he repeats after Buffon that cows shed their horns every third year.

'nalyse means:- to split up into
to components parts
lso to get at its true meaning
Criticise Goldsmith statement
of the Physical features, &
products of Switzerland

Make a List of leading
French author of Goldsmith
time and characterise their
influence upon subsequent
European thought and action
Diderot, Rousseau
Voltaire, Beaumarchais
D'Alembert)

Johnson 7 Chamier
Goldsmith 8 Nugent
Burke
Langton
Hawkins
Beauclerc

in the dedication: "The undertaking a comedy, not merely sentimental, was very dangerous; and Mr. Colman, who saw this piece in its various stages, always thought it so." So true was this, that Colman, probably remembering the failure of *The Good-natured Man*, was induced only by the most importunate solicitations of Goldsmith's friends to give it a trial. But the play was at once a success, and has ever since held its ground as an established favourite of the British public.

The story of the rest of Goldsmith's life is soon told. Even in comparative affluence he was not prosperous. It is calculated that in twelve months he received eighteen hundred pounds for his writings; yet he was never out of debt, and was perpetually moody and perturbed on account of money matters. He spent much in various pleasures, especially in his early vice of gambling. He spent more in charity, or in what seemed to him to be charity. His ears, heart, and purse, were alike open to any tale of distress; he was simple, credulous, impulsive as a child, and kept by his liberality an army of compatriot scribblers out of well-merited penury. His literary labours were unremitting. His last design was to publish *An Universal Dictionary of the Arts and Sciences*, to which all his literary friends were to contribute articles on the subjects with which they were most familiar; but this design was interrupted by his last illness. Two short poems, *The Haunch of Venison* and *Retaliation*, with some other fugitive verses, were written about this time, and published after his death.

In the spring of 1774 a malady to which his spasmodic fits of sedentary work made him specially liable attacked him with unusual violence; aggravating circumstances produced fever; on March 25th the case was serious; the patient persisted, contrary to the advice of his physicians, in doctoring himself; and he died on April 4th, aged 45.

Goldsmith was buried in the Temple burying-ground, and his friends raised a subscription for his monument in Westminster Abbey, and a large medallion by Nollekens, with an inscription by Dr. Johnson,* was placed in the Poets' Corner, between the monuments of Gay and the Duke of Argyle.

The face on this medallion is said to be a tolerably good likeness of Goldsmith; but the mere bodily features are in his case the least interesting part of the man. His face, which in his early childhood had given little promise of beauty, had been fearfully disfigured by the small-pox when he was eight years old; the wan, sickly child grew into a pale-faced, pock-marked, ungainly boy, and these characteristics he always retained; in figure, thick-set and clumsy; in face, uninteresting even to ugliness. Yet these physical defects had doubtless considerable influence in shaping the character of the man. As a child, he was shy; as a youth, proud; as a man, sensitive. Half the anecdotes which have been told in disparagement of Goldsmith have been due either to his ill-governed pride or his morbid self-consciousness. His discontent with his position as sizar at Dublin, his dissatisfaction with his tutorship at the Duke of Hamilton's, where he fancies himself "liked more as a jester than companion," his incurable objection to the subordinate situation of an usher may be traced to the former; while his sensitive disposition rendered him unfit to shine in society, especially in the society of the Turk's Head, where the imperious tyranny of Johnson, though genial and considerate to him personally, and the petty self-conceit and jealousy of Boswell, "the arch malice of Garrick, and the polished sneer of Beauclerk," must have combined to stifle all the little conversational power which he possessed. This same

* This epitaph contains the famous eulogium, "Qui nullum fere scribendi genus non tetigit, nullum quod tetigit non ornavit."

Refer to Historical event
in proof of the bravery and
patriotism of the Dutch
in the time of Cromwell
" their war with Spain
" " " " France

If line 333 be taken to mean
that the English peasant
exercised the right of
franchise how far is it correct
[illegible]

He was the laughing-stock
of the club

Examine the statements
made in lines 375-376

The trading Periodicals to
which Goldsmith contributed

1. Monthly Review
2. Literary Magazine
3. Critical Review
4. Bee
5. Lady's Magazine
6. The Busy Body
7. British Magazine
8. Public Ledger
9. Christian's Magazine

What les events to the time
probably suggested to the
poet the ifamous expres
in the lines 38/75

quality laid him open to charges of vanity and envy; for, as Mr. Forster remarks, "Too little self-confidence begets the forms of vanity;" and a self-conscious man betrays by word or look the passing feeling which a man of greater self-control more prudently conceals. Another curious trait connected with his external peculiarities was his love of finery in dress. One fact which he never forgot was that he was a gentleman; and yet he was conscious that nature had scarcely given him the appearance of gentility. Consequently he tried to compensate for the defect by striking, but too often laughable, effects in dress; and from the time when the scarlet breeches secured for him his rejection as a candidate for Orders, to the purchase of the peach-blossom coat which prompted Garrick's sarcasms, this eccentricity was always exposing him to ridicule.

But if he was quick to take offence, he was even quicker to pardon; if he was ready to feel, and even to show a transient bitterness or jealousy, he was far more ready to love those who were kind to him, and to sympathize with the distressed. He was always open-hearted and open-handed; equally incapable of niggardliness and dissimulation; to give and to forgive came naturally to him. Of course there were some who failed to appreciate him, and accordingly felt no compunction in making the sensitive nature of "little Goldy" the theme of unfeeling jokes, and more who had no scruple in playing off their impostures on his unsuspicious and indiscriminate generosity. Let us then make the most of his faults; let us say the worst we can of the disappointing indolence and "masterly thoughtlessness" of his youth, and of the incorrigible improvidence and provoking weakness of his whole life; but all this cannot for a moment be balanced against the virtues which have made him the most loving, loveable, and loved of British writers. Sympathy, generosity, unselfishness, gentleness, and purity of feeling; these were the qualities that won the hearts of the worthiest of his contemporaries, and have endeared him to all succeeding generations; which made Burke burst into tears, and Reynolds desert his studio, on hearing of his death, and prompted Johnson to say to the recording Boswell: "Let not his failings be remembered; he was a very great man;" which crowded his staircase in the Temple with weeping outcasts, while the coffin was re-opened that the lovely Mary Horneck might obtain a lock of his hair. They loved him as men love a gifted, affectionate, though sometimes wayward, child; we love him as an example of genius in its most innocent, kind-hearted, and attractive guise.

In what then does the special charm and attraction of Goldsmith's writings consist? The answer is threefold: it lies partly in his diction, partly in his subjects, partly in his mode of treating his subjects.

His language is always singularly refined: just as in society he never forgot that he was a gentleman, so in writing he never forgot what was due to himself and what to his readers. Composing with consummate ease, he is never vulgar; handling the most familiar subjects, he never condescends to buffoonery or loses his self-respect. Again, his style is particularly clear and luminous: many of his sentences we read twice over; but it is not to remove an obscurity, but to deepen our admiration of the thought or expression. But though his words are happily chosen, with little apparent effort, or straining after effect, he cannot be acquitted of occasional negligence and carelessness; though never vulgar, he is sometimes slipshod.

Deficient in imagination, but excelling in observation, Goldsmith selected his subjects from within the range of his own experience; though this is more or less true of many writers, perhaps of all, and especially true of Eng-

on the
"Didactic Poetry"

E Lane.

Actors — Garrick, Foote
Dramatists — Home, Mason, Congreve
Poets — Johnson, Pope, Thompson, Cowper
Novelists — Fielding, Richardson, Smollet
Historians — Hume, Robertson, Gibbon

lish novelists, who, from Fielding to Dickens, have made themselves the heroes of their own novels, it applies to Goldsmith in a pre-eminent degree. It would be possible, with a small exercise of ingenuity, to reconstruct his character out of his works by the light of internal evidence; and not only his own, but the characters of the more prominent members of his family. Indeed he was a close and accurate observer of the men and things around him, yet neither penetrative nor scientific. The short poem, *Retaliation*, is sufficient proof of his powers of observation, where the sketch of Edmund Burke is quite inimitable; but he had little imagination. When he proceeds beyond the limits of his personal experience, instead of rising, like Shakespeare, to his most wonderful creations, he becomes ineffective; thus the delineation of the horrors of the tropics, in *The Deserted Village*, is tawdry and inexpressive compared with the familiar picture of Irish desolation. *The Vicar of Wakefield* is imperfect as a sketch of English provincial life, but has created for us at least one character which will never die. It was this same defect which made Goldsmith fail lamentably as a critic; for he gave his warmest admiration to those works which appealed least to the imagination. He had little sympathy with Shakespeare or Milton, and preferred Tickell to Thomson, Parnell to Gray. Another result was that the ideas with which he had to work were limited in number: his characters reappear in new dresses, and even his images are often repeating themselves. But within this limited range he was supreme. Just as a great general with a small but well-drilled army will accomplish more than more numerous troops under inferior leadership, so Goldsmith, from the absolute control in which he held his intellectual forces was more effective than many other writers who cannot discipline the exuberant and fantastic creations of their brain.

Lastly, in the treatment of his subjects he was, as Dr. Johnson describes him in his epitaph, "Sive risus essent movendi, sive lacrymæ, affectuum potens, sed *lenis* dominator:" in all his humour there is pathos, and in his pathos humour. True to nature, he knows that smiles and tears are separated by no wide interval; and his comedy never degenerates to farce, nor his sentiment to sentimentality. His fidelity to nature forms perhaps his chief title to the position of a great poet; a fidelity, exhibited not only, as we have seen, in the delineation of a character, but also in the details of a description. In this he presents a marked contrast to his contemporary Gray, who depicts nature as seen through the mirror of books or of classical phrases; the recluse of the university cloister is seen in every line, while with Goldsmith we feel that we are in the company of one who has wandered amid all sorts of scenery and mixed in all kinds of society, and who reproduces his genuine impressions at first hand.

To sum up his strength and weakness, he was at his best "naturae minister et interpres," and yet "tantum facit et intelligit quantum de naturae ordine re vel mente observaverit : nec amplius scit aut potest."

d

a list of Goldsmith's
cal & prose works
the History of the Reduction
, and pt. out the
ue of its publication of

It contained
as sentiments.

"THE TRAVELLER:"

OR, "A PROSPECT OF SOCIETY."

INTRODUCTION.

THIS poem was originally published in quarto, and made its appearance on December 19, 1764: the date it bears is 1765. Goldsmith had been engaged upon it for a long time. It is certain that a rough sketch of part of it had been previously sent by the poet to his brother Henry, probably during his travels in Switzerland; and it is not unlikely that other parts were designed, if not actually written, during his travels. At last the poem was completed by the advice of Dr. Johnson, who himself added some of the closing lines. The poet received twenty guineas for it from the publisher, Newbery. Its success at its first appearance was not instantaneously striking; but in eight months it ran through four editions. Johnson declared that it was the greatest poem which had appeared since the days of Pope; and it is said that he had been seen to weep over the lines which describe the English character. At any rate, in a short time the fame of Goldsmith was established; and it was felt that a new poet had arisen among the literary men of the capital.

The Traveller was dedicated by the poet to his brother, Rev. Henry Goldsmith. One or two sentences of the dedication must be quoted : " It will throw a light upon many parts of it " (*sc.* the poem) " when the reader understands that it is addressed to a man who, despising fame and fortune, has retired early to happiness and obscurity, with an income of forty pounds a year. I now perceive, my dear brother, the wisdom of your humble choice. You have entered upon a sacred office, where the harvest is great, and the labourers are but few; while you have left the field of ambition, where the labourers are many, and the harvest scarce worth carrying away..... Poetry makes a principal amusement among unpolished nations; but in a country verging to the extremes of refinement, painting and music come in for a share. As these offer the feeble mind a less laborious entertainment, they at first rival poetry, and at length supplant her, they engross all that favour once shown to her, and, though but younger sisters, seize upon the elder's birthright. . . . What reception a poem may find which has neither abuse, party, nor blank verse to support it, I cannot tell, nor am I solicitous to know. My aims are right. Without espousing the cause of any party, I have attempted to moderate the rage of all. I have endeavoured to know that there may be equal happiness in states that are differently governed from our own, that each state has a particular principle of happiness, and that this principle in each may be carried to a mischievous success.",

Throughout the poem two characters are visible—the exile, wandering in foreign lands and sighing for his country, to which distance is lending its enchantment; and the political philosopher, inculcating his paradoxical theory that one form of government is as conducive to human happiness as another. With Goldsmith in his former character all must thoroughly sympathize. He is always charming when he is drawing on the rich stores of his personal experience; and here his own individuality seems to inspire his criticisms and his complaints. But to Goldsmith as a political philosopher we must take exception. Though it is true that under the best of governments some men would probably remain miserable, while under the worst some few may attain to happiness, it is far more true that some forms of government do more for the happiness of the individual than others. A government conducted with a view to the greatest good of the greatest number may possibly make mistakes, and occasionally defeat its own objects; but it will at any rate be more productive of happiness than the rule of a selfish and irresponsible Oriental despot, a ποιμὴν λαῶν, who regards his subjects as his flock, to be fleeced or devoured at his pleasure.

When was blank verse introduced into E. poetry.

Select lines beginning
'trochees or spondees

THE TRAVELLER.

REMOTE, unfriended, melancholy, slow,
Or by the lazy Scheld, or wandering Po;
Or onward, where the rude Carinthian boor
Against the houseless stranger shuts the door,
Or where Campania's plain forsaken lies, 5
A weary waste expanding to the skies;
Where'er I roam, whatever realms to see,
My heart untravelled fondly turns to thee;
Still to my brother turns, with ceaseless pain,
And drags at each remove a lengthening chain. 10

Eternal blessings crown my earliest friend,
And round his dwelling guardian saints attend:
Blest be that spot, where cheerful guests retire
To pause from toil, and trim their evening fire:
Blest that abode, where want and pain repair, 15
And every stranger finds a ready chair:
Blest be those feasts with simple plenty crowned,
Where all the ruddy family around
Laugh at the jests or pranks that never fail,
Or sigh with pity at some mournful tale; 20
Or press the bashful stranger to his food,
And learn the luxury of doing good.

But me, not destined such delights to share,
My prime of life in wandering spent and care:
Impelled with steps unceasing to pursue 25
Some fleeting good, that mocks me with the view;

That, like the circle bounding earth and skies,
Allures from far, yet, as I follow, flies;
My fortune leads to traverse realms alone,
And find no spot of all the world my own. 30

E'en now, where Alpine solitudes ascend,
I sit me down a pensive hour to spend;
And, placed on high above the storm's career,
Look downward where a hundred realms appear—
Lakes, forests, cities, plains extending wide, 35
The pomp of kings, the shepherd's humbler pride.

When thus creation's charms around combine,
Amidst the store should thankless pride repine?
Say, should the philosophic mind disdain
That good which makes each humbler bosom vain? 40
Let school-taught pride dissemble all it can,
These little things are great to little man;
And wiser he whose sympathetic mind
Exults in all the good of all mankind. 44
Ye glittering towns with wealth and splendour crowned;
Ye fields where summer spreads profusion round;
Ye lakes whose vessels catch the busy gale;
Ye bending swains that dress the flowery vale;
For me your tributary stores combine:
Creation's heir, the world, the world is mine! 50

As some lone miser, visiting his store,
Bends at his treasure, counts, recounts it o'er;
Hoards after hoards his rising raptures fill,
Yet still he sighs, for hoards are wanting still:
Thus to my breast alternate passions rise, 55
Pleased with each good that Heaven to man supplies:
Yet oft a sigh prevails, and sorrows fall,
To see the hoard of human bliss so small;
And oft I wish, amidst the scene, to find
Some spot to real happiness consigned. 60
Where my worn soul, each wandering hope at rest,
May gather bliss, to see my fellows blest.

But, where to find that happiest spot below,
Who can direct, when all pretend to know?

Deo Rule (Rules) Plectin Plectrus Plei
Roam (Roma) A seque exp ind simile
Chain Catena Crown Imperative mood
Eternal (Eternus) Feed Expento
Crown coronal

It Sanctua Lucus is like
Clear Cathedra Forest Loris—
fest festum out of doors
Altars altar a pomp pomp
Realms Regnum Sheep lie
dedain disdain
Charm Carmen Vain Vanus
School Scho'i Exult Exulto

A set me down is asker karsin)
An Epizeuxis as a word repeated
for the sake of emphases)
Asyndeton is the absence of
the connecting conjunction)

A Metonomy is one word used
for another as (sorrow for
tears)

(Strong is an analogy of
an antithesis)

(Zeugma – a word repeated at beginning ~~palin~~
Epanalepsis) (i: taking up again
(Alliteration, beginning with s is
a signature us)

Woods over Woods / Compared with
the seats in a theatre is
a metaphor) H?L
(Nature's Bounty. Personification)

THE TRAVELLER.

The shuddering tenant of the frigid zone   65
Boldly proclaims that happiest spot his own;
Extols the treasures of his stormy seas,
And his long nights of revelry and ease;
The naked negro, panting at the line,
Boasts of his golden sands and palmy wine,   70
Basks in the glare, or stems the tepid wave,
And thanks his gods for all the good they gave.

Such is the patriot's boast, where'er we roam,
His first, best country, ever is at home.
And yet, perhaps, if countries we compare,
And estimate the blessings which they share,
Though patriots flatter, still shall wisdom find
An equal portion dealt to, all mankind;
As different good, by art or nature given,
To different nations makes their blessings even.   80

Nature, a mother kind alike to all,
Still grants her bliss at labour's earnest call;
With food as well the peasant is supplied
On Idra's cliff as Arno's shelvy side;
And though the rocky-crested summits frown,   85
These rocks, by custom, turn to beds of down.
From art more various are the blessings sent—
Wealth, commerce, honour, liberty, content.
Yet these each other's power so strong contest,
That either seems destructive of the rest.
Where wealth and freedom reign, contentment fails,
And honour sinks where commerce long prevails.
Hence every state, to one loved blessing prone,
Conforms and models life to that alone.
Each to the favourite happiness attends;   95
And spurns the plan that aims at other ends;
Till, carried to excess in each domain,
This favourite good begets peculiar pain.

But let us try these truths with closer eyes,
And trace them through the prospect as it lies: 100
Here, for a while my proper cares resigned,
Here let me sit in sorrow for mankind;
Like yon neglected shrub, at random cast,
That shades the steep, and sighs at every blast.

Far to the right, where Apennine ascends, 105
Bright as the summer, Italy extends:
Its uplands sloping deck the mountain's side,
Woods over woods in gay theatric pride;
While oft some temple's mouldering tops between
With venerable grandeur mark the scene. 110

Could nature's bounty satisfy the breast,
The sons of Italy were surely blest.
Whatever fruits in different climes were found,
That proudly rise, or humbly court the ground;
Whatever blooms in torrid tracts appear, 115
Whose bright succession decks the varied year;
Whatever sweets salute the northern sky
With vernal lives, that blossom but to die;
These here disporting own the kindred soil,
Nor ask luxuriance from the planter's toil; 120
While sea-born gales their gelid wings expand
To winnow fragrance round the smiling land.

But small the bliss that sense alone bestows,
And sensual bliss is all the nation knows.
In florid beauty groves and fields appear, 125
Man seems the only growth that dwindles here.
Contrasted faults through all his manners reign:
Though poor, luxurious: though submissive, vain;
Though grave, yet trifling; zealous, yet untrue;
And even in penance planning sins anew. 130
All evils here contaminate the mind,
That opulence departed leaves behind;
For wealth was theirs, not far removed the date, from
When commerce proudly flourished through the state;
At her command the palace learned to rise, 135
Again the long-fallen column sought the skies,
The canvas glowed, beyond e'en nature warm,
The pregnant quarry teemed with human form;
Till, more unsteady than the southern gale,
Commerce on other shores displayed her sail; 140
While nought remained of all that riches gave,
But towns unmanned and lords without a slave:
And late the nation found with fruitless skill
Its former strength was but plethoric ill.

Comparing Commerce to sail is
: metaphor

My and is a personification
Climes for Climate ice meteorory
~~Two lines~~ begining with the
same word is an aporth-
chills the lack of new hero mit...

Yet still the loss of wealth is here supplied 145
By arts, the splendid wrecks of former pride:
From these the feeble heart and long-fallen mind
An easy compensation seem to find.
Here may be seen, in bloodless pomp arrayed,
The pasteboard triumph and the cavalcade: 150
Processions formed for piety and love,
A mistress or a saint in every grove:
By sports like these are all their cares beguiled;
The sports of children satisfy the child;
Each nobler aim, represt by long control, 155
Now sinks at last, or feebly mans the soul;
While low delights, succeeding fast behind,
In happier meanness occupy the mind:
As in those domes, where Cæsars once bore sway,
Defaced by time and tottering in decay, 160
There in the ruin, heedless of the dead,
The shelter-seeking peasant builds his shed;
And, wondering man could want the larger pile,
Exults, and owns his cottage with a smile.

    My soul, turn from them, turn we to survey 165
Where rougher climes a nobler race display,
Where the bleak Swiss their stormy mansion tread,
And force a churlish soil for scanty bread;
No product here the barren hills afford
But man and steel, the soldier and his sword; 170
No vernal blooms their torpid rocks array,
But winter lingering chills the lap of May;
No zephyr fondly sues the mountain's breast,
But meteors glare, and stormy glooms invest.

    Yet still, even here, content can spread a charm, 175
Redress the clime, and all its rage disarm.
Though poor the peasant's hut, his feast though small,
He sees his little lot the lot of all;
Sees no contiguous palace rear its head,
To shame the meanness of his humble shed; 180
No costly lord the sumptuous banquet deal,
To make him loathe his vegetable meal;
But calm, and bred in ignorance and toil,
Each wish contracting, fits him to the soil,

Cheerful at morn, he wakes from short repose, 185
Breathes the keen air, and carols as he goes;
With patient angle trolls the finny deep;
Or drives his venturous ploughshare to the steep;
Or seeks the den where snow-tracks mark the way,
And drags the struggling savage into day. 190
At night returning, every labour sped,
He sits him down the monarch of a shed;
Smiles by his cheerful fire, and round surveys
His children's looks, that brighten at the blaze;
While his loved partner, boastful of her hoard, 195
Displays her cleanly platter on the board:
And haply too some pilgrim, thither led,
With many a tale repays the nightly bed.

    Thus every good his native wilds impart
Imprints the patriot passion on his heart; 200
And e'en those hills, that round his mansion rise,
Enhance the bliss his scanty fund supplies.
Dear is that shed to which his soul conforms,
And dear that hill which lifts him to the storms;
And as a child, when scaring sounds molest, 205
Clings close and closer to the mother's breast,
So the loud torrent, and the whirlwind's roar,
But bind him to his native mountains more.

    Such are the charms to barren states assigned;
Their wants but few, their wishes all confined. 210
Yet let them only share the praises due,
If few their wants, their pleasures are but few;
For every want that stimulates the breast
Becomes a source of pleasure when redrest.
Whence from such lands each pleasing science flies, 215
That first excites desires, and then supplies;
Unknown to them, when sensual pleasures cloy,
To fill the languid pause with finer joy;
Unknown those powers that raise the soul to flame,
Catch every nerve and vibrate through the frame. 220
Their level life is but a smouldering fire,
Unquenched by want, unfanned by strong desire;
Unfit for raptures, or, if raptures cheer
On some high festival of once a year,

Content disarm rage is a personification / personifying.
Afford Ir affored to set a pro
Steel is a metonomy (170)
Soldier Solidus derivation
Torpid means barren (171)
May Dev Majores (172) om

January from Janus a God of beg
February Februa
March from Mars
April from Aperu
June " Juniores
July " Julius
August " Agustes
October " Octo eight
November " Noven nine

A spardijo-feil is a a letter or syllable added to the end of a word

An Onomatopoeia is the sound resembling the sense

In wild excess the vulgar breast takes fire, 225
Till, buried in debauch, the bliss expire.
But not their joys alone thus coarsely flow :
Their morals, like their pleasures, are but low ;
For, as refinement stops, from sire to son,
Unaltered, unimproved, the manners run ; 230
And love's and friendship's finely-pointed dart
Fall, blunted, from each indurated heart.
Some sterner virtues o'er the mountain's breast
May sit, like falcons cowering on the nest ;
But all the gentler morals, such as play 235
Through life's more cultured walks, and charm the way,
These, far dispersed, on timorous pinions fly,
To sport and flutter in a kinder sky.

To kinder skies, where gentler manners reign,
I turn ; and France displays her bright domain. 240
Gay sprightly land of mirth and social ease,
Pleased with thyself, whom all the world can please,
How often have I led thy sportive choir,
With tuneless pipe, beside the murmuring Loire !
Where shading elms along the margin grew, 245
And freshened from the wave the zephyr flew ;
And haply, though my harsh touch faltering still,
But mocked all tune, and marred the dancer's skill ;
Yet would the village praise my wondrous power,
And dance, forgetful of the noontide hour. 250
Alike all ages. Dames of ancient days
Have led their children through the mirthful maze,
And the gay grandsire, skilled in gestic lore,
Has frisked beneath the burden of threescore.

So blest a life these thoughtless realms display ; 255
Thus idly busy rolls their world away.
Theirs are those arts that mind to mind endear,
For honour forms the social temper here ;
Honour, that praise which real merit gains,
Or even imaginary worth obtains, 260
Here passes current ; paid from hand to hand,
It shifts in splendid traffic round the land :
From courts to camps, to cottages it strays,
And all are taught an avarice of praise ;

They please, are pleased, they give to get esteem, 265
Till, seeming blest, they grow to what they seem.

But while this softer heart their bliss supplies,
It gives their follies also room to rise ;
For praise too dearly loved, or warmly sought,
Enfeebles all internal strength of thought : 270
And the weak soul, within itself unblest,
Leans for all pleasure on another's breast.
Hence ostentation here, with tawdry art,
Pants for the vulgar praise which fools impart ;
Here vanity assumes her pert grimace, 275
And trims her robes of frieze with copper lace ;
Here beggar pride defrauds her daily cheer,
To boast one splendid banquet once a year :
The mind still turns where shifting fashion draws,
Nor weighs the solid worth of self-applause. 280

To men of other minds my fancy flies,
Embosomed in the deep where Holland lies.
Methinks her patient sons before me stand,
Where the broad ocean leans against the land ;
And, sedulous to stop the coming tide, 285
Lift the tall *rampire's* artificial pride. [*rampart*
Onward, methinks, and diligently slow,
The firm connected bulwark seems to grow,
Spreads its long arms amidst the watery roar,
Scoops out an empire, and usurps the shore— 290
While the pent ocean, rising o'er the pile,
Sees an amphibious world beneath him smile ;
The slow canal, the yellow blossomed vale,
The willow-tufted bank, the gliding sail,
The crowded mart, the cultivated plain— 295
A new creation rescued from his reign.

Thus, while around the wave-subjected soil
Impels the native to repeated toil,
Industrious habits in each bosom reign,
And industry begets a love of gain. 300
Hence all the good from opulence that springs,
With all those ills superfluous treasure brings,
Are here displayed. Their much-loved wealth imparts
Convenience, plenty, elegance, and arts ;

bigger for faggarty is an ekph-
analogy, an antinomia
an hypotyposis or vision
animated description

{Salt
Zunge} Name of Lakes referred
Tjurke} to in line (3/2):-

feebly (flebili lamantalele)(*les nap*
combat (combattre)
fermento (*fermes to boil*)

But view them closer, craft and fraud appear, 305
Even liberty itself is bartered here.
At gold's superior charms all freedom flies;
The needy sell it, and the rich man buys:
A land of tyrants, and a den of slaves,
Here wretches seek dishonourable graves, 310
And, calmly bent, to servitude conform,
Dull as their lakes that slumber in the storm.

Heavens! how unlike their Belgic sires of old—
Rough, poor, content, ungovernably bold,
War in each breast, and freedom on each brow; 315
How much unlike the sons of Britain now!

Fired at the sound, my genius spreads her wing,
And flies where Britain courts the western spring;
Where lawns extend that scorn Arcadian pride,
And brighter streams than famed Hydaspes glide. 320
There, all around, the gentlest breezes stray;
There gentlest music melts on ev'ry spray;
Creation's mildest charms are there combined:
Extremes are only in the master's mind.
Stern o'er each bosom Reason holds her state, 325
With daring aims irregularly great.
Pride in their port, defiance in their eye,
I see the lords of human kind pass by,
Intent on high designs, a thoughtful band,
By forms unfashioned, fresh from nature's hand, 330
Fierce in their native hardiness of soul,
True to imagined right, above control;
While even the peasant boasts these rights to scan,
And learns to venerate himself as man.

Thine, freedom, thine the blessings pictured here, 335
Thine are those charms that dazzle and endear;
Too blest, indeed, were such without alloy,
But fostered e'en by freedom, ills annoy;
That independence Britons prize too high,
Keeps man from man, and breaks the social tie: 340
The self-dependent lordlings stand alone,
All claims that bind and sweeten life unknown.—
Here, by the bonds of nature feebly held,
Minds combat minds, repelling and repelled;

Ferments arise, imprisoned factions roar, 345
Repressed ambition struggles round her shore.
Till, overwrought, the general system feels
Its motions stopped, or frenzy fire the wheels.

Nor this the worst. As nature's ties decay,
As duty, love, and honour fail to sway, 350
Fictitious bonds, the bonds of wealth and law,
Still gather strength, and force unwilling awe.
Hence all obedience bows to these alone,
And talent sinks, and merit weeps unknown;
Till time may come, when, stripped of all her charms,
The land of scholars, and the nurse of arms, 355
Where noble stems transmit the patriot flame,
Where kings have toiled, and poets wrote for fame,
One sink of level avarice shall lie,
And scholars, soldiers, kings, unhonoured die. 360

Yet think not, thus when freedom's ills I state,
I mean to flatter kings, or court the great.
Ye powers of truth, that bid my soul aspire,
Far from my bosom drive the low desire!
And thou, fair freedom, taught alike to feel 365
The rabble's rage, and tyrant's angry steel;
Thou transitory flower, alike undone
By proud contempt, or favour's fostering sun,
Still may thy blooms the changeful clime endure!
I only would repress them to secure; 370
For just experience tells in ev'ry soil,
That those who think must govern those that toil;
And all that freedom's highest aims can reach
Is but to lay proportioned loads on each.
Hence, should one order disproportioned grow, 375
Its double weight must ruin all below.

O then how blind to all that truth requires,
Who think it freedom when a part aspires!
Calm is my soul, nor apt to rise in arms,
Except when fast approaching danger warms; 380
But, when contending chiefs blockade the throne,
Contracting regal power to stretch their own,
When I behold a factious band agree
To call it freedom when themselves are free;

factious (facis to make)
ambition,
general, (generalis)
system, (systema)
frenzy (phren the mind)
decay, (de + cado to fall)
duty, (debeo ~~douse~~ I. owe)
honor, honneur
ail, hallo
fictitious, fictus, famed
force, fortis, strong

line (346) Mike escaped from Britain and went to France
Fictitious means not genuine 35.1
Asyndeton is the absence of the connecting conjunction

394) refers to Charles I & Cromwell
401 & 2
(401 & 2) people emigrate and
the land becomes depopulated
Opulence is obj to so said.
Melas Black & Cole Bile
They thought that melancholy
was caused by black Bile
History of Melancholy
The Thesis of the Deserted Village
(405 - 410) enclusive
Tangled forests is a metaphor 414

THE TRAVELLER.

Each wanton judge new penal statutes draw,
Laws grind the poor, and rich men rule the law;
The wealth of climes, where savage nations roam,
Pillaged from slaves to purchase slaves at home;
Fear, pity, justice. indignation start,
Tear off reserve, and bare my swelling heart; 390
Till half a patriot, half a coward grown,
I fly from petty tyrants to the throne.

Yes, brother! curse with me that baleful hour
(When first ambition struck at regal power;)
And, thus polluting honour in its source,
Gave wealth to sway the mind with double force.
Have we not seen, round Britain's peopled shore,
Her useful sons exchanged for useless ore?
Seen all her triumphs but destruction haste,
Like flaring tapers brightening as they waste? 400
Seen opulence, her grandeur to maintain,
Lead stern depopulation in her train,
And over fields where scattered hamlets rose,
In barren so........
Have we not seen........ordly call, 405
The smiling, long-frequented village fall?
Beheld the duteous son, the sire decayed,
The modest matron, and the blushing maid,
Forced from their homes, a melancholy train,
To traverse climes beyond the western main; 410
Where wild Oswego spreads her swamps around,
And Niagara stuns with thundering sound?

Even now, perhaps, as there some pilgrim strays
Through tangled forests and through dang'rous ways,
Where beasts with man divided empire claim, 415
And the brown Indian marks with murderous aim;
There, while above the giddy tempest flies,
And all around distressful yells arise,
The pensive exile, bending with his woe,
To stop too fearful, and too faint to go, 420
Casts a long look where England's glories shine,
And bids his bosom sympathise with mine.

Vain, very vain, my weary search to find
That bliss which only centres in the mind.

C

Why have I strayed from pleasure and repose, 425
To seek a good each government bestows?
In every government, though terrors reign,
Though tyrant kings or tyrant laws restrain,
How small, of all that human hearts endure,
That part which laws or kings can cause or cure! 430
Still to ourselves in every place consigned,
Our own felicity we make or find.
With secret course, which no loud storms annoy,
Glides the smooth current of domestic joy;
The lifted axe, the agonising wheel, 435
Luke's iron crown, and Damiens' bed of steel,
To men remote from power but rarely known,
Leave reason, faith, and conscience, all our own.

The lines written × were written by Samuel Johnson

made throne, Surrounding throne so
-ing the king from absolute power
tending Chiefs, Pitt, Bute, Grenville
anton unchecked (385)
Vimes, Africa, Lydia (388)
(12 & 395) means :— The poets patriotism
rises on account of his fear for
the future he appeals to the
throne

Repetition — of a word is epizeuxis
centrum is from kentron
" sharp point

prose works of G.
To
D. Village } prose
Hermit. }
part of J. was written in Italy
Go shewed it to J. and he
advised its publication

G. Dramatic Works
The stoops to conquer
Good natured man
Poeta Laureate
it his
Whitehead

NOTES

THE TRAVELLER.

The Argument.

(1-10) The poet assures his brother, to whom he dedicates the poem, of his affection for him, an affection that no distance can efface, no variety weaken; and (11-22) invokes blessings on his quiet, hospitable home. (23-30) Far different is the lot of the wandering poet, who after long journeyings (31-36) takes his place on some Alpine height, and moralizes on the scene below, (37-50) in the spirit not of an unsympathetic or cynical philosopher, but of an open-hearted philanthropist, (51-58) and with feelings as mixed as those of the miser counting his gold— with satisfaction with what has been gained, sorrow that so much is absent.

(58-62) The poet longs to find some abode of perfect happiness on earth. (62-80) Esquimaux and negro, in fact all patriots, claim it for their own country, and for equally good reasons; (81-98) for everywhere life may be sustained, everywhere the blessings of civilization are counteracted by disadvantages.

(99-104) Let us prove this by induction. (105-110) Take: I. Italy, its natural beauty, (111-122) and luxuriant fertility. (122-144) But the character of the people is a compound of all the faults that the prosperity and subsequent collapse of commerce could produce, (145-164) with just enough artistic taste to cripple nobler energies. (165-175) II. Switzerland. Though the soil is barren, and the climate severe, (175-198) yet, as all are poor, all are contented. The life has its own homely joys; (199-208) so that the Swiss loves his country the more for its lack of natural advantages. (209-226) But this rough life incapacitates him for the enjoyment of the more refined forms of pleasure, (227-238) or for the practice of the gentler virtues. (239-254) III. France. The people are of a happy disposition, (255-266) every man eager to gain the good opinion of the circle in which he moves; (267-280) but this naturally results in a want of independence, and in an ostentatious sham. (281-296) IV. Holland. The very nature of the country, rescued with difficulty from the ocean, (297-300) inculcates industry and thrift; (301-312) but a universal venality is the natural accompaniment of these qualities. (313-316) A sad degeneration! (317-334) V. Britain. The country favoured by nature, the inhabitants free, independent, high-spirited, 'the lords of human kind.' (335-348) But independence begets disunion, political and social; (349-360) and repressive measures develop the coarser forces of society at the expense of the finer, so as to threaten national degeneracy.

(361-376) The evils of freedom should be plainly stated, and its true nature settled to be a proportionate adjustment of the burdens of society, (377-392) and not the ascendancy of any one class; *e.g.* of an aristocratic clique which defies the crown; (392-422) for as loyalty decreases, the predominance of wealth increases, and the rich man drives the poor to exile on a distant and perilous shore.

(423-438) But the search for perfect government is at once futile and unimportant; for governments affect but very slightly the happiness of individuals.

1 *Remote.* More commonly used of places than of persons. Cf. l. 437.

Melancholy. (Gr. μέλας, black, and χολή, bile). One of a large family of words; *e.g.* 'humour,' 'humourous,' 'choleric,' 'sanguine,' &c., which have their origin in an old theory of medicine, "according to which there were four principal moistures or 'humours' in the natural body, on the due proportion and combination of which the disposition alike of body and of mind depended." Cf. Trench, *Study of Words,* lect. iii.

Slow. "'Chamier,' said Johnson, 'once asked me what he (Goldsmith) meant by *slow,* the last word in the first line of *The Traveller.* Did he mean tardiness of locomotion?' Goldsmith, who would say something without consideration, answered, 'Yes.' I was sitting by, and said, 'No, sir; you do not mean tardiness of locomotion. You mean that sluggishness of mind which comes upon a man in solitude.' Chamier believed I had written the line as much as if he had seen me write it."—BOSWELL, *Life of Johnson.*

2 *Lazy Scheld.* A river in the N. of France and W. of Belgium, flowing by Tournay, Oudenarde, Ghent, Antwerp.

Wandering Po. A river in the N. of Italy, rising in the Alps, passing by Turin, Piacenza, Cremona, and emptying itself by many mouths into the Adriatic.

3 *Carinthian.* Carinthia, a province of the Austrian Empire between Illyria and Styria, visited by Goldsmith in 1755.

of hymn — have we seen the green woodside
  oer oer the heath, we herd our labourers
  it has the woodlark piped his farewell song
  with wistful eyes pursue the setting sun
      2nd 5th stanza
contrast Blessings of Nature
  & Art 81 & 88

Essence is an imperfect
rhyme
The p. has des. the climate and
productions of S. in order to
make a more striking contrast
Adam Smith. Economist
Home Tone & The Idler
Scott Nover Vicar of Wakefield
Loster Irving Prior have
  written Biographies of G

NOTES.

Boor. A word adopted from the Dutch 'boer,' literally 'a husbandman,' akin to Ger. 'bauen,' 'to till.' For the degradation of meaning cf. 'knave,' 'varlet,' 'pagan,' 'villain,' &c.

5 *Campania.* A province of Central Italy, bounded on the north by Latium, and on the south by Lucania: celebrated in classical times for its extraordinary fertility.

Forsaken. In spite of the contrast between the past and present condition of some of its towns (*e.g.* Capua), it is still one of the most populous provinces of Italy.

7 *Realm.* Through Old Fr. 'realme,' from a late Lat. form 'regalimen.'

8 *Untravelled.* Cf. the address of a lover to his mistress in Ford's well-known madrigal—

"Where beauty moves, and wit delights,
And signs of kindness bind me;
There, oh, there, where'er I go,
I leave my heart behind me."

10 *And drags at,* &c. Goldsmith often repeats his images. So (*vide* Aldine edition) "The farther I travel I feel the pain of separation with stronger force. Those ties that bind me to my native country and you are still unbroken; by every remove I only drag a greater length of chain."
—*Citizen of the World,* vol. i. lett. iii.

11 *Crown.* Optative = 'may eternal blessings crown.'

15 *Want and pain.* Abstract for concrete. Cf. l. 77.

Repair. This neuter verb, 'to go to,' differs in derivation as well as in meaning from the active verb meaning 'to mend or restore.' This is from Fr. 'repairer,' from late Lat. 'repatriare,' literally 'to re-visit one's native country,' while that is from Lat. 'reparare,' literally to 'prepare again.'

17 *Crowned.* This metaphorical use is common in all periods; *e.g.*

"This grief is crowned with consolation."
—SHAKESPEARE, *Antony and Cleop.*
"Crown a happy life with a fair death."
—TENNYSON, *Enid.*

18 *Ruddy; i.e.* the hue of health.

19 *Jests.* Originally a deed or exploit; Lat. 'gestum,' from 'gero,' 'to do.' Hence in mediæval language the narration of anything interesting or amusing.

Prank. 'A trick,' an old word, though of doubtful derivation, perhaps from Welsh 'pranc,' a frolic, or akin to Dutch 'pronk,' 'ostentation,' 'finery,' and probably to 'prance.'

22 *Luxury,* &c. Cf. Rogers' *Pleasures of Memory*—"This truth once known, to bless is to be blest."

23 '*Me.*' This objective case is governed by 'leads' in l. 29.

THE TRAVELLER.

24 *My prime*, &c. An absolute clause explanatory of l. 22. *In wandering spent and care.* Not an uncommon variation of the natural order of the words. Cf. Waller's *Ode to the Lord Protector*—"Justice to crave, and succour, at your court."

26 *Fleeting.* Probably akin to the substantive 'fleet,' so originally 'floating swiftly away.' Cf. also adjective 'fleet,' substantive 'fleetness.'

That mocks me, &c. Man's prospects of happiness have often been compared to a mirage.

27 *The circle; i.e.* the horizon (τὸ ὁρίζον) or boundary line.

28 *Allures; i.e.* as being apparently near.

32 *Sit me down.* Many verbs now used intransitively were once reflexive; so 'I repent me,' 'I fear me.' Notice that poetry preserves archaic forms.

33 *Placed on high above*, &c. That such a position may be often literally true, is the experience of all who have explored the higher mountains. Cf. of the Alps in Rogers's *Pleasures of Memory*—

"Though far below the forked lightnings play,
And at his feet the thunder dies away."

Career. 'The course which the storm takes,' literally a 'road for a car,' from Fr. 'carrière.'

35 *Lakes*, &c. These substantives are added to explain and are in opposition to 'a hundred realms.'

36 *Pomp.* Used in a sense very far removed from its original one of 'sending,' from Gr. πέμπω (Cf. *D. V.* l. 66, 259), and = 'pride' in this line, 'that which gives rise to feelings of pride.'

38 *Store; i.e.* abundance. Derived from Lat. 'instauro,' 'to renew,' through Old Fr. 'estoire.'

40 *Vain.* The poet does not use this condemnatory epithet, but puts it in the mouth of the philosopher. But the poet here mistakes the true spirit of philosophy, which echoes rather the cry of the slave-dramatist Terence, "Homo sum, nihil humani a me alienum puto."

41 *School-taught; i.e.* taught in the schools of philosophy. All mediæval philosophers were roughly classed as 'schoolmen,' and their philosophy was termed 'scholastic.' Cf. Pope's *Epistle to Arbuthnot*—"Unlearned, he knew no schoolman's subtle art." And on scholasticism cf. Hallam's *Middle Ages*, part ii. chap. ix.

Dissemble. From Lat. 'dissimulare,' 'to disguise or conceal.'

42 *These little things; i.e.* those which 'make each humbler bosom vain.'

43 *Wiser; i.e.* than philosopher or schoolman.

Sympathetic. 'Sympathy,' from Gk. σύν, 'together,' πάθος, 'feeling.' So identical in meaning with 'com-passion' or 'fellow-feeling.'

born 1728, son of Westmeath
village school, small pox,
Elphin, Athlone, Edgeworthstown
Trinity College D, BA 1749
teacher, clergyman, lawyer, Physic
Edinburgh, Leyden, London
Green Arbour Court Islington
Wakefield. Dr. Mr. Vicar
died 1774

NOTES.   55

45 *Crowned.* This repetition of one word (as in lines 11, 17) is characteristic of Goldsmith. Cf. 'realms' in lines 7, 29, 34, and 'stranger' in lines 16, 21, and 'bend' in 48, 52.

47 *Busy; i.e.* 'restless.'

48 *Bending; i.e.* 'stooping to their work.'

Dress. Lit. 'to make straight.' So 'to put or keep in order,' 'to deck.' From Lat. 'dirigere.' So 'a vine-dresser.'

49 *Tributary; i.e.* 'all contributing to form one pleasing whole.'

50 *Creation's hair.* Cf. Cowper's *Task. The Winter Morning*, l. 738-741—

"He looks abroad into the varied field
Of nature; and though poor, perhaps, compared
With those whose mansions glitter in his sight,
Calls the delightful scenery all his own."

Read the whole passage.

51 *Store.* How far is its meaning in this line different from its sense in l. 38?

52 *Recounts.* In its literal sense, 'counts again.'

54 *Yet still he sighs.* The insatiability of misers has been a common-place in all ages. "Crescit amor nummi quantum ipsa pecunia crescit."—JUVENAL. "Multa petentibus desunt multa."—HORACE. Cf. Lord Lytton's *My Novel*, bk. x.—"Philus," saith a Latin writer, "was not so rich as Lælius; Lælius was not so rich as Scipio; Scipio was not so rich as Crassus; and Crassus was not so rich as he wished to be."

56 *Pleased.* This agrees with the personal pronoun implied in the word 'my' in the line before.

57 *Prevails.* In the literal sense, 'gets the mastery.'

Sorrows fall. It seems more natural to make this phrase mean, 'sorrows fall upon or oppress the heart,' than to wrest 'sorrows' into meaning 'tears of sorrow.'

60 *Consigned.* 'Assigned' or 'appropriated.'

63 *To find.* Dependent on 'direct,' in l. 64.

65 *Frigid zone.* Gk. ζώνη, a girdle or belt. Geographers have divided the earth into five great divisions: the torrid zone, situated between the tropics; the two temperate zones; and the two frigid zones, enclosed within the polar circles.

68 *Long nights.* In the most northern parts of Lapland the sun remains below the horizon from November 20th to January 10th.

69 *The line; i.e.* the equator, an imaginary line dividing the earth into the northern and southern hemispheres.

70 *Golden sands.* The Gold Coast.

Palmy wine. This is made from the sap of the Palmyra palm, the cocoa-nut palm, and many other species.

THE TRAVELLER.

71 *Glare.* The hot, bright sunlight. The word is akin to 'clear,' and Lat. 'clarus.'

72 *Gave.* 'Have given' would have been the more natural termination of the clause, if the sequence of tenses was followed out; but Goldsmith was often not too particular. Cf. l. 113, and *Deserted Village*, l. 92.

73, 74 For such boasts, and the moral naturally drawn from them, see Longfellow's ballad, *The Happiest Land*, translated from the German.

77 *Wisdom.* Cf. l. 15.

79 *Good; i.e.* advantages.

81 *Nature, a mother.* Turn the metaphor into a simile.

83 *Peasant.* 'One who lives in the country (as opposed to the town).' Derived from Fr. 'paysan,' from 'pays,' 'country.' Lat. 'pagus,' a 'village' or 'district' (whence 'pagan').

84 *Idra's cliff.* Idra, or more properly Idria, is in Carniola, a district of Illyria, situated partly on several low hills, partly at the bottom of a narrow valley surrounded by high mountains, on the banks of the little river Idria. It is famous for its quicksilver mines.

Arno. A river in Tuscany. What towns are on it?

Shelvy side; i.e. 'abounding in shelves, shoals, or shallows.'

85 *Rocky-crested.* A compound epithet = 'crested with rocks.'

Frown. A very common metaphor for the threatening aspect of cliffs, crags, &c. Cf. Byron's *Childe Harold*, canto iii.—

"The castled crag of Drachenfels
Frowns o'er the wide and winding Rhine."

This is called by Abbott a personal metaphor; a personal relation is transferred to an impersonal object.

86 *Rocks by custom.* The force of habit makes the rocks as comfortable as feather-beds. So Locke calls custom "a greater power than nature."

87 *Art.* Used, of course, in its wider sense, as in 'artificial,' not in 'artistic.'

88 *Content.* The usual substantive (as in l. 91) is contentment. But cf. note on *D. V.* l. 413, and—

"Nought's had, all's spent,
Where our desire is got without content."
—SHAKESPEARE, *Macbeth*, act iii. sc. 2.

89 *Strong.* Used for adverb 'strongly,' 'powerfully.' Cf. "The moon shines bright."

90 *Either.* Properly only one of two, and not, as here, one of five.

91 *Contentment fails.* Freedom being shared by the many; wealth by the few.

92 *Honour sinks.* The low tone of commercial morality is the unfailing subject of laments in every age.

93 *Prone.* 'Inclined,' literally 'bending forwards.' For the sentiment cf. Pope's *Essay on Man*, l. 131-2—
"And hence one Master Passion in the breast,
    Like Aaron's serpent, swallows up the rest"—
with the thirty lines which follow.

96 *Spurns.* 'Rejects,' 'throws aside.' Cf. *D. V.* l. 106.

97 *Domain.* Here merely 'country,' usually 'an estate.' From Lat. 'dominium,' 'the estate' of, 'dominus,' 'the master' of, 'domus,' 'a house.' Another form of the word is 'demesne.'

98 *Peculiar pain.* Some evil specially arising from the excessive development of this characteristic. As every virtue carried to excess becomes a vice, so every pleasure over-stimulated becomes a pain. Cf. Gray's *Ode on the Pleasure of Vicissitude*—
"Still where rosy pleasure leads
  See a kindred grief pursue."

101 *Proper.* As Lat. 'proprius,' Fr. 'propre,' 'peculiar to oneself,' 'personal.'

103 *Like yon neglected shrub,* &c. Such is the position of the melancholy traveller-poet, as he looks down from his Alpine solitudes.

105 *Apennines.* The general name for the great mountain system of Italy, divided into four sections, the Ligurian, Etruscan, Roman, and Neapolitan Apennines. The highest of them is Monte Corno, 9,521 feet.

108 *Woods over woods.* In apposition to 'uplands.'

Theatric. As in a theatre, a place for sights. From Gk. θεάομαι, 'I view.' Cf. "Silvis scena coruscis."—VIRGIL, *Æn.* i. 164. Is it flattering to nature to compare her works with those of the scene-painter?

111 *Could,* &c. The praises of Italy have often been sung by poets. Cf. Virgil, *Georgic* ii. 136-176; Addison's *Letter from Italy;* or, as a longer description, Rogers' *Italy,* and especially Byron's *Childe Harold,* canto iv.

113 *Were found.* The present tense would be more natural. Cf. l. 72.

114 *Court the ground.* A natural metaphor for the creeping plant.

115 *Torrid.* Cf. on l. 65.

118 *Vernal lives.* 'Short as the spring-time.'

119 *Own.* 'Acknowledge,' like 'confess' in *D. V.* l. 76.

Kindred soil. Just the same metaphor as in 'congenial.'

120 *Ask,* &c. 'Require the planter's toil to produce luxuriant growth.'

121 *Gelid.* 'Cold,' 'cool,' scarcely naturalized in English (Lat. 'gelidus'). But (cf. Thomson's *Summer,* l. 205—"By

gelid founts and careless rills to muse") common enough in poetry of the last century.

122 *Winnow fragrance.* This figure sounds somewhat far-fetched. 'To scatter fragrance over the land, as the winnowing-machine scatters the chaff.' Cf. the use of the verb in Milton's *Par. Lost*, v. 269—"Then with quick fan winnows the buxom air."

123 *Sense; i.e.* 'the senses.'
125 *Florid.* 'With profusion of flowers.'
127 *Manners.* Used in a deeper sense than mere 'manners.' Cf. Lat. 'mores.'
Cf. "And give us manners, virtue, freedom, power."
—WORDSWORTH, *Sonnet to Milton.*

129 *Zealous ; i.e.* enthusiastic for religion. Cf. *Spectator*, No. 185—"I would have every zealous man examine his heart thoroughly, and I believe he will often find that what he calls a zeal for his religion is either pride, interest, or ill-nature."

131 *Contaminate; i.e.* 'corrupt by contagion.'
133 *Not far removed the date; i.e.* 'in comparatively recent times.'
Date. Literally 'the time when any document was *given* or issued.' Cf. the form used now in official papers—"*Given* at our court, &c., this 19th day," &c.

134 *Commerce.* Venice, Florence, Genoa, Pisa were the chief seats of Italian commerce, probably the wealthiest, certainly the most refined towns of Europe in the 15th century.

135 *Learned to rise.* Cf. l. 85. But the present hardly amounts to a personal metaphor ; for 'learnt' = was taught, was made.

136 *Long-fallen; i.e.* since the days of Roman greatness.

137 *Canvas.* 'Hempen cloth' (from Lat. 'cannabis,' 'hemp'), specially used for painting. Cf. Addison's *Letter from Italy*—
"A nicer touch to the stretched canvas give,
Or teach their animated rocks to live."
And sails. Cf. Waller's *Ode to the King on his Navy*—
"Where'er thy navy spreads her canvas wings
Homage to thee, and peace to all she brings."

Beyond e'en nature warm. A phrase applicable most closely perhaps to Titian (Tiziano Vecellio, a Venetiân, born in 1477), of all the great Italian painters.

138 *The pregnant*, &c. Cf. Rogers's *Pleasures of Memory*—
"Who from the quarried mass, like Phidias, drew
Forms ever fair, creations ever new."
But the phrase is here far fetched, for the quarry teems with human form ; *i.e.* contains statues *in posse*, as much at one time as another.

139 *Southern gale.* Why southern? Perhaps because the south wind brings storms, and hence is considered as gusty or fitful.

140 *On other shores.* Chiefly owing to the spread of maritime discovery, which opened new channels for trade.

142 *Unmanned.* In the literal sense of 'depopulated,' very rarely so used, except of ships. What is the usual sense?

143 *Skill.* Used in the archaic sense of knowledge. So the verb, "All that could skill of instruments of music."—2 *Chron.* xxxiv. 12.

144 *Plethoric.* 'Plethora' is a medical word, 'overfulness of blood' (from Gr. πληθέω, 'to be full'). So 'plethoric' here means 'overgrown or overfull to an extent that produced an unhealthy state.' For a description of this cf. *The Deserted Village*, l. 389-394.

147 *Long-fallen.* Notice the repetition of this epithet from l. 136.

150 *Pasteboard triumph.* This probably is an allusion to the drolleries of the Carnival. For instance, at Rome "the carriages and horses are decked out in a very fine or a very capricious manner." Thus a "coachman, dressed as a Spanish cavalier of the olden times, is driving an old Tabellone, or notary, with a huge wine-flask (extended towards a Punch on stilts), and a Roman doctor, with 'spectacles on nose,' while a small-grown Punch climbs up the side-steps, and a full-grown Punchinello, with a squeaking trumpet to his lips, and a sturdy, turbaned Moor act as footmen." Or again at Naples, large cars are decked out as ships, and drawn up the Toledo by six horses or oxen, manned with sham sailors, who furl or unfurl the sails, or discharge larboard and starboard volleys of sugar-plums. Cf. MacFarlane's *Popular Customs of the South of Italy*.

Cavalcade. This may refer to the races of riderless horses in the Corso at Rome at the time of the Carnival. The animals are spurred on by leaden balls with steel spikes attached to their girths; and no less a personage than the governor of Rome was the judge of the race. Or perhaps the allusion is to pageantry got up in imitation of a mediæval hunting party, or some similar scene.

154 *The sports of children*, &c. Who does not know the charming story of Sir Joshua Reynolds surprising Goldsmith engaged in teaching his dog to beg, while on his desk beside him was lying the unfinished MS. of the *Traveller*, the ink of this line still wet?

156 *Mans.* Carries on the metaphor of a vessel.

159 *Domes.* 'Palaces.' Cf. *D. V.* l. 319. Often used for any high and spacious hall; and not in its commoner, though narrower, sense of a hemispherical structure raised above the roof of a building. Thompson uses the word similarly for the nest of birds (*Spring*), hives of bees (*Autumn*), &c.

162 *Shelter-seeking.* This epithet is inserted to bring the simple object of the peasant into prominence.

165 *My soul, turn,* &c. In all this description of Switzerland, there is no conception of its beauty, which now attracts to it millions of admirers every year. The love of wildness in nature has grown up since Goldsmith's time. He was himself one of the few Saxons who had then ventured to explore the Highlands; but, disgusted by the hideous wilderness, he declared that he greatly preferred Holland. Scotland "presented a dismal landscape;" "hills and rocks intercepted every prospect;" how great a contrast to the country round Leyden; "nothing can equal the beauty" of the latter, with its "fine houses, elegant gardens, statues, grottos, vistas." Cf. Macaulay's *History of England,* ch. xiii.

167 *Bleak Swiss.* An epithet oftener applied to places than to persons, originally meaning 'pale,' rather than 'exposed,' 'unsheltered.' It is akin to the verb 'to bleach.'

Mansion. Cf. *D. V.* l. 140. Here rather 'an abiding-place,' 'a home,' as a district, than 'a house.'

168 *Force the soil.* 'Extract the scanty produce from it not without great difficulty and labour.'

Churlish. 'Ill-natured,' 'surly;' but not seldom applied to things; *e.g.* "Spain found the war so churlish and longsome."— BACON. "In Essex they have a very churlish blue clay."— MORTIMER, *Husbandry.* Originally a churl meant merely 'a country fellow.' A.S. 'ceorl.' Cf. Scotch 'carle.'

170 *Soldier and his sword.* The monument at Lucerne, by Thorwaldsen, commemorates the most famous exploit of the Swiss as mercenaries.

171 *Torpid.* 'Inactive,' 'incapable of the exertion of producing anything.' So Lat. 'torpentes gelu.'

Array. Derived from Fr. 'arroi,' which is either a hybrid word from 'ad' and Teutonic 'rât,' 'counsel,' 'help;' or from Low Lat. 'arraia,' from Ger. 'reihe,' a 'row.' But had Goldsmith never seen or heard of gentians and Alpine roses?

173 *Zephyr.* Soft west wind.

Sues. (Fr. 'suivre,' 'to follow,' Lat. 'sequor.') Phrases which speak of the wind 'wooing' or 'kissing' are perhaps more common than this; but the metaphor is the same.

174 *Meteor.* Properly 'anything suspended above us' (from Gr. μετέωρος), 'any atmospheric phenomenon,' not necessarily fiery or bright; *e.g.* with Aristotle dew is a meteor.

Invest. Here in its literal sense, 'to cover up with a dress.' (Lat. 'vestis,' 'a robe.')

176 *Redress the clime.* Cf. l. 214.

179 *Contiguous.* 'Touching,' 'adjoining,' from Lat. 'contingo' ('con,' 'tango,' 'I touch'). Cf. *D. V.* l. 179.

Palace. From the Palatine, one of the Seven Hills of Rome, on which Augustus had his residence.

181 *Banquet.* From Fr. 'banquet,' Italian 'banchetto,' 'a little bench' or 'table,' diminutive of 'banco,' originally from an Old High German word 'banc.'

183 *Calm.* Especially as being free from envy and avarice.

184 *Each wish.* Objective case after the participle 'contracting,' which agrees with the nominative to 'fits.' "By narrowing his wants, and limiting his desires, he suits himself to his country." Cf. l. 382. Cf. Horace—"Contracta melius parva cupidine Vectigalia porriges," &c.

186 *Carols.* 'Sings,' from Fr. 'carole,' Italian 'carola.'

187 *Angle.* Now more commonly used as a verb. But cf. Shakespeare's *Ant. and Cleop.* act. ii. sc. 5—"Give me mine angle; we'll to the river." The angle was properly the hook (Cf. 'angle' as meaning 'a corner'), but used for rod, line, and hook together.

Trolls. Akin to the words 'roll,' 'drill,' &c., properly applied to the rotatory motion, as the line passes over the reel. Cf. 'to troll a catch or round,' a piece of music in which the same air is passed round to each singer in succession.

'*Trolls the deep.*' It is rather a forced construction, as the line, if anything, is that which is trolled.

Finny deep. It seems a violent figure of speech to transfer the epithet from the fish to the sea. Would 'the antlered forest' or 'the feathered grove' be equally admissible? Cf. however 'the warbling grove,' *Deserted Village*, l. 361.

188 *Venturous.* 'Adventurous' is the more usual form.

Ploughshare. The portion of the plough which divides the soil. Connect together 'shear,' 'share,' 'shire,' 'sheer,' 'shore,' 'shred,' 'sherd,' 'short;' and give any other words of the same family. Cf. Trench, *Study of Words*, lect. vi.

Steep; i.e. 'up the steep hill-side.'

190 *Savage.* The bear. Rarely used as a substantive except of human beings. Literally 'an inhabitant of the woods.' From Fr. 'sauvage,' Italian 'selvaggio,' Lat. 'silvaticus,' from 'silva,' a wood. For this sense cf. Pope's *Iliad*, xviii. 373, of a lion—

"When the grim savage, to his rifled den
Too late returning, snuffs the track of men."

191 *Sped.* Participle of 'to speed;' here 'accomplished successfully,' without any notion of quickness, just as in the proverb, "More haste, worse speed."

192 *Sits him down.* For this use of 'him' cf. l. 32.

193 *Smiles by his cheerful*, &c. Quote a parallel passage from Gray's *Elegy.*

196 *Platter.* Collect and connect as many words as possible which are etymologically allied to this.

197 *Haply.* Adverb formed from the substantive 'hap'= 'chance.'

Pilgrim. Literally 'a man who goes through countries.' (Lat. 'per,' 'ager.' So 'peregrinus,' and Italian 'peregrino,' 'pellegrino,' and 1 r. 'pelerin.')

198 *Nightly.* 'For the night;' not, as usually, 'for a succession of nights.'

200 *Patriot.* Used, as often, for an adjective. Cf. l. 357.

202 *Enhance.* 'Heighten.' Derivation from Lat. 'ante,' 'before.' So 'en avant,' 'forwards;' thence was formed Provençal 'enansar,' 'to advance.'

203 *Conforms.* 'Suits itself.'

205 *Scaring.* 'To scare' is properly 'to drive away by frightening,' as in the phrase 'scare-crow.' So 'to frighten' generally.

211 *Share.* Not used very accurately. They obtain all, and not a mere share of the praises that are really due.

213 *Stimulates.* From Lat. 'stimulus,' 'a goad.' 'Spurs or goads it on.' Their pleasures are as few as their wants, as they are merely the satisfaction of those wants. Cf. the ancient definition of ἡδονή as ἀναπλήρωσις τῆς ἐνδείας.

215 *Whence* = 'consequently.' The mind is too sluggish to allow new desires to be created in it.

217 *Cloy.* 'To glut,' 'satiate.' Probably akin to 'clog.'

218 *To fill.* This infinitive is the subject to 'is unknown.' What would be the prose construction?

Languid pause. The natural reaction after sensual excess.

220 Notice the confusion of metaphors. Expand them into similes.

221 *Level.* 'Even,' 'unvaried,' 'monotonous.' Cf. l. 359.

Smouldering. Burning very slowly, producing more dust than flame. Some copies read 'mouldering.'

224 *Of once a year.* 'Of' gives an adjectival force to the phrase (cf. 'of gold' = 'golden'); 'once' is treated as a substantive, governed by 'of.' Cf. 'A child of one year old.'

226 *Debauch.* A metaphor from masonry; literally 'a deviation from the straight line.' (From 'de' and Old Fr. 'bauche,' 'a row of bricks.')

Expire. Observe the mood.

227 *Alone.* This use of the word, though common, is scarcely correct. 'Not only their joys.'

231 *Dart.* The dart or shaft of love is a very common metaphor, which Molière laughed at, and which is now confined to valentines and crackers. It is very naturally transferred to friendship.

232 *Indurated.* Hardened (from Lat. 'durus,' 'hard'). 'Obdurate' is perhaps a more common compound.

Fall. The plural cannot be grammatically correct, though the construction is easily explained.

Cf. "Grief, mixed with pity, in our bosoms *rise*."—CRABBE.

234 *Cowering.* This word, though not here, generally implies the notion of fear.

236 *Charm the way* = 'beguile the length or monotony of the journey of life.'

241 *Sprightly.* 'Spright' or 'sprite' is but another form of 'spirit.' Is it not the Frenchman's boast that his is the land of 'esprit'?

242 *Whom all,* &c. The poet illustrates the characteristic of being easily pleased by his own success. (Lines 247-250.)

243 *Choir.* This word here reverts to its original sense, 'a band of dancers.' Gk. χορός, Lat. 'chorus.'

244 *Tuneless.* We may hope the poet exaggerates his own deficiencies.

Loire. Rises in the Cévennes, and falls into the Atlantic after a course of 530 miles. Through what provinces and by what towns does it flow?

245 *Margin.* Any 'edge' or 'border.' Not uncommon in this sense in poetry.

247 *Faltering.* 'Failing,' 'being at fault.' From Lat. 'fallo.'

248 *But.* 'Only.' Cf. the Latin idiom, 'nihil (facere) nisi.'

249 *Village.* The place put for the inhabitants; *e.g.* "the talk of the town."

251 *Dame.* From Lat. 'domina,' 'the mistress of a household;' Fr. 'dame.'

252 *Maze.* A word of uncertain derivation; perhaps akin to 'miss.' As a description of a dance, the word is common enough.

253 *Gestic lore; i.e.* dancing. Cf. 'gesture,' 'gesticulation.'

256 *Idly busy.* Not an uncommon instance of 'oxymoron.' Cf. the Latin phrase, "Operose nihil agendo," and Horace's "Strenua nos exercet inertia." Pope's *Elegy on an Unfortunate Lady*—

"Life's idle business at one gasp be o'er."

World. In what sense is this word used here?

258 *Forms the social; i.e.* regulates the temper of society. By honour is here meant not the internal principle, but the outward distinction.

261-264 Honour is the coinage recognized or valued in society. The metaphor, like most metaphors, will not bear to be pushed very far.

262 *Traffic.* From Italian 'trafficare,' probably from Lat.

"'trans,' 'beyond,' and 'facere,' 'to do.' So 'trade done beyond the seas.'
   Cf.   "Exercent alii socii commercia linguae."
                          —OVID, *Tristia*, v. x. 35.
   264 *Avarice of praise.* So Horace describes the Greeks, *Ars Poetica*, 324—
            "Praeter laudem nullius avaris."
   265 *They please.* "They exert themselves to please others, and are pleased at the success of their efforts, so winning the esteem and good opinion of society; hence they seem to themselves happy. And what more is required for them to be so, except the continuance of this till it becomes habitual?"
   270 *Thought.* The influence which France was soon to have, and was even then beginning to acquire, over the thought of Europe, seems not to have been foreseen by Goldsmith. He is as unconscious as Johnson was of the existence of D'Alembert, Diderot, and Beaumarchais.
   273 *Ostentation* ; **275**, *Vanity* ; **277**, *Pride*, are here personified. These personifications are a note of eighteenth century poetry.
   273 *Tawdry.* Said to be derived from St. Audrey or St. Ethelreda, as at fairs on that saint's day gewgaws of various sorts were sold. It had not always a depreciatory sense.
   275 *Pert* had at first no bad sense; probably akin to 'pretty.'
   Grimace. Perhaps originally 'a *grim* look ;' but more probably from Old Scandinavian, 'grima,' 'a mask.'
   276 *Frieze.* 'The curling nap on cloth.' So 'any coarse kind of woollen cloth.' Connected with 'to frizz' of hair, or 'frizzle,' or Fr. 'friser.' "The word gets its sense in architecture from the idea of 'frizzled work ;' and so 'any kind of border.'"—LATHAM. But Rev. I. Taylor (*Words and Places*, p. 291) derives 'frieze' as a cloth from Friesland, and as an architectural term from Phrygia.
   Copper. Polished so as to imitate gold.
   277 *Beggar' pride.* The snobbishness which stints itself of daily comforts, to boast an occasional entertainment in the style of a class socially superior, has been sufficiently satirized.
   Cheer. Connect the various meanings of this word.
   280 *Self-applause.* The satisfaction of a good conscience.
   282 *Embosomed.* A strong metaphor expressing the fact that much of the country lies actually below the sea-level.
   Holland. Derived either from 'ollant,' 'marshy ground' (Taylor's *Words and Places*, p. 55), or from Ger. 'hohl,' 'the hollow land.' Cf. 'hole.' A low-lying tract in Lincolnshire is also called Holland.
   283 *Methinks.* In this phrase 'me' is the dative, and 'thinks' is impersonal.

$\frac{1}{2}, \frac{3}{4}, \frac{5}{7}$ Let $\frac{y}{x} = y\,CM$

$\frac{1}{2} \times \frac{y}{x} =$ whole no.
$\frac{3}{4} \times \frac{y}{x} =$ "   "
$\frac{5}{7} \times \frac{y}{x} =$ "   "

x must divide 1.3.5.
y "   "   2.5.7

x must be as large as poss.
  $\therefore$ GCM of 1.3.5
y must be as small as poss.

$\therefore y = LCM$

NOTES.

Cf. "It thinketh me I sing as wel as thou."—CHAUCER.
285 *Sedulous*. In original meaning like 'assiduous,' 'sitting close to one's work' (from Lat. 'sedeo'). So 'diligent,' 'painstaking.'
286 *Rampire*. The commoner form of the word in modern English is 'rampart.' From Fr. 'rempart' ('se remparer,' 'to intrench oneself'). But this form is common enough in older writers ; *e.g.* Pope's and Dryden's translations—
"The Trojans round the place a rampire cast."
—DRYDEN, *Æneid*, vii. 213.
"So down the rampires rolls the rocky shower."
—POPE, *Iliad*, xii. 180.
288 *Bulwark*. Properly 'a defensive work made with the boles or trunks of trees.' Ger. 'bollwerk,' Fr. 'boulevard.' The Helder dyke is perhaps the best instance. Nearly two leagues long, it is forty feet broad at the top, where is an excellent road ; and it descends into the sea by a slope of 200 feet, at an angle of forty degrees. Huge buttresses project at certain intervals several hundred yards into the sea. It is built entirely of huge blocks of granite from Norway.
290 *Scoops out*; *i.e.* by keeping the sea to a higher level; not by excavating the land to a lower. So Marvell talks of the Dutch 'fishing the land to shore.'
291 *Pent*. Participle of 'to pen.' Cf. 'a sheep-pen.'
292 *Amphibious*. Usually of animals (from Gk. ἀμφί, 'around,' 'doubly,' βίος, 'life').
293 *Slow canal*. 'Sluggish,' 'whose waters have scarcely any motion.' Like 'lazy' of the Dutch Scheldt in l. 2.
Canal. From Lat. 'canalis,' 'a water-pipe;' from 'canna,' 'a reed.'
Yellow-blossomed. Probably the blooms of the tulips are meant.
295 *Mart*. Contracted from 'market,' Fr. 'marché,' Lat. 'mercatus,' from 'merx,' 'merchandise.'
296 *Rescued*, &c. Cf. Goldsmith's *Animated Nature*, i. p. 276—"Holland seems to be a conquest upon the sea, and in a manner rescued from its bosom." (Aldine edition.)
297 *Wave-subjected*. 'Subject to the waves so long as to be rendered sterile and unproductive,' or perhaps 'which lies beneath the level of the waves, so that the native is constantly employed in repairing the dykes.'
302 *With all those ills*, &c. The subject of much of the *Deserted Village*.
303 *Are*. For this plural cf. note on l. 232.
305 *Craft*. Had originally no bad sense. Cf. 'craftsman,' 'handicraft.'
306 *E'en liberty*. Cf. *Vicar of Wakefield*, ch. xix.—"Now

E

the possessor of accumulated wealth, when furnished with the necessaries and pleasures of life, has no other method to employ the superfluity of his fortune but in purchasing power; that is, differently speaking, in making dependants, by purchasing the liberty of the needy or the venal, of men who are willing to bear the mortification of contiguous tyranny for bread." Again, "in Holland, Genoa, or Venice, the laws govern the poor, and the rich govern the law."

309 *A land*, &c. This line occurs verbatim in the *Citizen of the World*, i.: "A nation once famous for setting the world an example of freedom is now become a land of tyrants and a den of slaves." (Aldine edition.)

311 *Bent.* 'Stooping to the yoke.'

313 *Belgic sires.* Batavic would be more correct. Who was Civilis?

315 *War . . . and freedom.* Is not this taunt undeserved? The history of the 16th and 17th centuries belies it.

317 *Genius spreads her wing.* English has no genders properly speaking. When, as here, sex is attributed to a personified abstraction, as a rule the gender of the language from which the word is taken is followed, but not uncommonly the gender is determined by another principle;—the sterner or more manly qualities, &c., are masculine, as 'honour,' 'courage,' 'death;' the milder, feminine, as 'faith,' 'hope,' 'beauty.' The gender of 'genius' in this passage seems anomalous.

319 *Lawns.* Cf. *D. V.* l. 35.

Arcadian pride. Before the time of Virgil, Arcadia was more celebrated for "pastoral dulness than pastoral ideality," as the proverbial expressions "Arcadici sensus," "Arcadicae aures" (cf. Juvenal, vii. 160) sufficiently show. They were a strong and hardy, but rude and savage race, in spite of the law, mentioned by Polybius, an Arcadian himself, which made the study of music compulsory. Since the days of Virgil (cf. *Eclogues*, vii. 4; x. 30), and especially since the revival of learning, Arcadia has become the golden land of poets and romance-writers. Who wrote the "Arcadia"? When?

320 *Hydaspes.* One of the principal rivers of the Punjaub. Its Sanscrit name was Vitastâ; its usual name in modern times, Jelum. It flows into the Chenab.

Famed. An epithet imitated from Horace, who calls the stream 'fabulosus' (*Odes*, bk. 1, xxii. 8), from the incredible stories narrated of it.

322 *Music melts.* A common metaphor.
   Cf. "The strains decay, and melt away
    In a dying, dying fall."
     —POPE, *Ode on St Cecilia's Day.*

Spray. This word is different from 'spray' in the sense of

NOTES. 67

small particles of water. It is rather akin to 'sprig,' a small shoot or branch.

324 *Extremes*, &c. This somewhat obscure line is explained by those which follow. Though extremes of climate or scenery are unknown, the minds of the owners of the soil are capable of extremes of daring (326), and of independence (331).

325 *Her state; i.e.* 'power,' 'sway.'

327 *Port.* 'Bearing' (from Lat. 'porto,' I bear or carry). Cf. Gray's *Bard*, iii. 2—"Her lion port, her awe-commanding face."

330 *Forms . . . nature's.* Cf. "Cursed be the sickly forms that err from honest nature's rule!"—TENNYSON, *Locksley Hall.*

332 *Imagined right.* What they think their privileges as Britons.

333 *To scan.* Literally 'to climb.' So 'to count the feet in a verse,' 'to scrutinize carefully;' here 'to examine closely, as if they belonged to himself.' 'Boasts to scan' for 'boasts the right to scan' is somewhat awkward.

335 *Thine, freedom*, &c. In thus putting forward freedom as the main point of contrast between England and foreign nations, the poet is following Addison in his *Letter written from Italy to Lord Halifax*—

"Oh, Liberty, thou goddess heavenly bright,
Profuse of bliss, and pregnant with delight!
* * * * * *
Thee, goddess, thee Britannia's isle adores."

But the courtly placeman does not impress on us the evils of freedom as vividly as the dissatisfied poet.

336 *Dazzle.* And so prevent the eye from steadily observing the effects.

337 *Alloy.* 'Some baser metal mixed with a finer.' From Fr. 'à la loi;' the proportions of such mixture for the purposes of coinage being regulated by law.

338 *But.* "But they are not without alloy; for fostered," &c.

341 *Lordling.* 'ling' is a common diminutive suffix; as in 'duckling,' 'gosling,' 'darling.'

344 *Minds combat.* Though members of one common country, the struggles of party are the condition of their independence.

345 *Ferments.* Agitation in politics, such as is produced by yeast in dough, or by the action of the air in certain liquids.

Imprisoned. 'Closely restrained within the bounds of law.' Illustrate this line from the history of the time.

347 *System.* Society as a connected whole, made up of various component parts.

348 *Motions . . . wheels; i.e.* of the machinery of society, the metaphor being slightly changed.

348 *Frenzy.* 'Madness;' from Gk. φρένησις (more common as Lat. 'phrenesis'), from φρήν, 'the mind.'
351 *Fictitious.* 'Artificial.'
357 *Stems.* Families.
Patriot flame. Cf. l. 200.
358 *Wrote.* A bye-form of 'written,' common in all periods of the language.
359 *Sink.* 'A drain into which refuse is poured or *sinks.*' This metaphorical use is common enough. Cf. the speech of the ship's captain to the Duke of Suffolk—

"Poole? Sir Poole? Lord?
Ay, kennel, puddle, sink; whose filth and dirt
Troubles the silver spring where England drinks."
—SHAKESPEARE, 2 *Henry VI.* iv. 1.

Level. Cf. l. 221.
363 *Ye powers of,* &c. This couplet recalls Pope's *Elegy on an Unfortunate Lady*—

"Why bade ye else, ye powers, her soul aspire
Beyond the vulgar flights of low desire?"

366 *Rabble.* 'A mob.' Originally 'raving;' akin to Lat. 'rabies.'
370 *To secure; i.e.* 'that I might secure them.'
372 *Those who think.* So far from 'just experience' teaching this, no nation has ever been governed by its thinkers. Plato's philosopher-king is still an unrealized ideal, though a Marcus Aurelius may have approximated to it. For a similar expression *vide* Thomson's *Seasons* (*Summer*)—

"While thus laborious crowds
Ply the tough oar, philosophy directs
The ruling helm."

374 *Is but to lay,* &c. No class is to be exempt. But with reference to what is the proportion to be assessed?
375 *Order.* 'Class in the state.'
377 *How blind,* &c. Understand 'are they.'
378 *A part,* &c. Freedom is something that all must share. It must not be the prerogative of a feudal aristocracy, or even of an Athenian democracy, denied to the lower strata of serfs or slaves.
380 *Warms.* An active verb, governing 'my soul,' understood from the previous line.
381 *Blockade.* 'Encircle the throne, so as not to allow either the royal mercy to reach the circles outside, nor the petitions of the humbler classes to reach the throne.'
382 *Contracting; i.e.* 'narrowing the limits of.' Cf. l. 284.
385 *Each wanton.* 'While each judge unscrupulously draws up fresh statutes, with severer punishments.'
386 *Rich men rule.* Cf. note on l. 306; also *Vicar of Wake-*

field, ch. xxvii.—"It were highly to be wished that legislative power would thus direct the law rather to reformation than severity; that it would soon be convinced that the work of eradicating crimes is not by making punishments familiar, but formidable." . . . "It is among the citizens of a refined community that penal laws, which are in the hands of the rich, are laid upon the poor. Government, while it grows older, seems to acquire the moroseness of age ; and as if our property were become dearer in proportion as it increased, as if the more enormous our wealth the more extensive our fears, all our possessions are paled up with new edicts every day, and hung round with gibbets to scare every invader." These were advanced views for Goldsmith's time.

388 *Pillage.* 'To plunder.' From Lat. 'pilo.'
390 *Tear off reserve; i.e.* 'abandon caution and concealment.'
392 *Petty.* Fr. 'petit.'
To the throne. Cf. the conclusion of the vicar's harangue in *Vicar of Wakefield*, ch. xix.
393 *Baleful.* 'Full of misery or woe.' 'Bale' is from A.S. 'bæl.'
394 *When first ambition*, &c. In all ages the worst foes to monarchical power have been the aristocracy. Thus in Greece the early tyrannies were almost universally overthrown by oligarchies. Cf. the barons' wars in English history, and the attitude of the crown towards the nobles in France.
395 *Polluting honour*, &c. It is one of the prerogatives of the crown to be the fountain of honour. Has it always been the fountain of that honour which Wordsworth describes as—
"The finest sense
Of *justice* which the human mind can frame,
Intent each lurking frailty to disdain," &c.?
396 *Gave wealth*, &c. ; *i.e.* gave wealth a double, because an undivided power, over the mind.
397 *Have we*, &c. Cf. *D. V.* l. 49-56.
398 *Her useful sons; i.e.* by emigration.
Ore. Metal in-an unworked state. From A.S. 'ore,' which in A.S. meant also the metal, and a coin worth from sixteen to twenty pence.
401 *Seen opulence*, &c. Cf. *D. V.* l. 63, 64.
403 *And over fields*, &c. Cf. *D. V.* l. 65, 66.
405 *Have we not*, &c. Cf. *D. V.* l. 275-282.
407 *Beheld the duteous*, &c. Cf. *D. V.* l. 362-384.
410 *Oswego.* A river which joins lakes Oneida and Ontario. There is a town of the same name near the place where it falls into Lake Ontario. The river is in the State of New York, and is sometimes called the Onondaga.
412 *Niagara.* Notice the accent falling on the penultimate.

412 *Stuns with thundering sound.* "'The noise is a vast thunder, filling the heavens, shaking the earth, and leaving the mind, although perfectly conscious of safety, lost and astonished. . . . Two gentlemen who had lived sometime at York, on the north side of Lake Ontario . . . informed me that it was not unfrequently heard there. The distance is fifty miles."—DWIGHT, *Travels in New England,* vol. iv. letter iv.

414 *Tangled forests.* Cf. *D. V.* l. 349.

415 *Where beasts.* Cf. *D. V.* l. 355.

416 *Marks.* Has here lost its transitive meaning. Cf. 'marksman.'

Murderous. Cf. *D. V.* l. 356.

417 *Giddy;* i.e. 'whirling round.'

418 *Distressful yells.* 'Cries of distress.' 'Yell,' like 'howl,' or Lat. 'ululo,' is formed from the sound.

420 *To stop too fearful.* This line was written by Dr. Johnson. *Vide* Boswell's *Life of Johnson,* ch. xix., under the year 1766: "In the year 1783, he, at my request, marked with a pencil the lines which he had furnished, which are only line 420 and the concluding ten lines, except the last couplet but one. He added, 'these are all of which I can be sure.' They bear a small proportion to the whole."

423 *Vain;* i.e. because the poet has been trying to discover, in the external conditions of climate, government, &c., the abode of happiness; and that after all 'centres in the mind;' *i.e.* 'is dependent on internal conditions.'

426 *A good each.* For happiness and freedom may be attained under any form of government. (Cf. Pope's *Essay on Man,* ii. 303—

"For forms of government let fools contest;
Whate'er is best administered is best.")

Or even, as Goldsmith shows, in spite of the greatest maladministration. *Vide* Introduction.

429 *How small,* &c. Cf. note on l. 420.

434 *Glides the smooth current.* Dr. Johnson was thinking of Horace's "Secretum iter et fallentis semita vitæ."

435 *Wheel.* "*Breaking on the wheel.* This barbarous mode of death is of great antiquity. It was used for the punishment of great criminals, such as assassins and parricides, first in Germany. It was also used in the Inquisition, and rarely anywhere else, till Francis I. ordered it to be inflicted upon robbers, first breaking their bones by strokes with a heavy iron club, and then leaving them to expire on the wheel."—HAYDN, *Dict. of Dates.* Allusions to it are common enough in the poets. Cf. Pope's *Epistle to Dr. Arbuthnot,* 308—

"Who breaks a butterfly upon a wheel?"

436 *Luke's iron crown.* "Goldsmith himself was in a mis-

take. In the *Respublica Hungarica* there is an account of a desperate rebellion in the year 1514, headed by two brothers of the name of *Zeck*, George and Luke. When it was quelled, *George*, not *Luke*, was punished by his head being encircled with a red-hot iron crown, 'coronâ candescente ferreâ coronatur.'"—BOSWELL, *Life of Dr. Johnson*, ch. xix. The name of the leaders of this peasant revolt was Dosa, not Zeck; and George Dosa was punished by being seated on a red-hot iron throne, with red-hot crown and sceptre; his veins were then opened, and he had to drink a glass of his own blood. He was then torn to pieces, and roasted; and his flesh was given as food to his principal supporters, who had been purposely famished.—*Biographie Universelle*.

Damiens. On January 5th, 1757, Damiens stabbed Louis XV. in his right side, as he was getting into his carriage at Versailles. Though the wound was very slight, and Damiens insisted that his intention was not to kill the king, but to frighten him and give him a warning, he was most barbarously tortured, and at the end of March was executed. His right hand was burnt off, his arms and legs torn with red-hot pincers, and melted lead, boiling oil, wax, resin, &c., poured into the wounds; and finally four horses were half an hour in pulling him limb from limb.

437 *Remote.* Cf. l. 1.

Known. This participle agrees with the nominatives in lines 435, 436. Notice that the logical nominative of the sentence is 'the lifted axe, &c., but rarely known;' *i.e.* 'the almost total absence of the lifted axe,' &c.

Miller & Co.'s English School Classics.

GRAY'S ELEGY,

—EDITED—

WITH JOHNSON'S LIFE, AND NOTES

—BY—

FRANCIS STORR, M.A.,

CHIEF MASTER OF MODERN SUBJECTS AT MERCHANT TAYLOR'S SCHOOL.

TORONTO:

ADAM MILLER & CO.

1879.

Sam. T Coleridge,
The Ancient Mariner,
Ode to the Departing Year,
Christabel

W Wordsworth, The Borde[rers?]
The Excursion, The White
Doe of Rylstone, Peter Bell

Lord Macaulay,
Lays of Ancient Rome.
History of England.

A Tennyson, Timbuctoo
The Princess, In Memori[am]
Idylls of The King
The Maud etc..

LIFE OF GRAY.

From Dr. Johnson's "Lives of the most eminent English Poets."

THOMAS GRAY,[1] the son of Mr. Philip Gray,[2] a scrivener[3] of London, was born in Cornhill, Novem-

---

[1] He was the fifth child of twelve children—eleven died in infancy from fulness of blood, and the poet owed his life to his mother's nerve, who, with her own hand, opened a vein.

[2] Philip Gray was a worthless father and a brutal husband, as we learn from a case submitted to counsel by Mrs. Gray, to ask whether her husband had any power to molest her in the business of milliner, which she was carrying on with her sister, or to compel her to live with him. The case states that she "almost provided everything for her son whilst at Eton School, and now he is at Peterhouse at Cambridge." Before his death his father had, besides attempting to ruin his family, nearly ruined himself by neglect of business and reckless expenditure in building a country house.

Gray's love of his mother in life, and his devotion to her memory, form perhaps the most pleasing trait in his character. In the epitaph he wrote for her monument he describes her as "the careful, tender mother of many children, one of whom only had the misfortune to survive her;" and in a letter to Mr. Nicholls, dated 1766, he writes: "It is long since I heard you were gone in haste into Yorkshire on account of your mother's illness, and the same letter informed me that she was recovered; otherwise I had then wrote to you, only to beg you would take care of her, and to inform you that I had discovered a thing very little known, which is, that in one's whole life one can never have any more than a single mother. You may think this is obvious, and what you call a trite observation. You are a green gosling! I was at the same age very near as wise as you, and yet I never discovered this (with full evidence and conviction I mean) till it was too late. It is thirteen summers ago, and seems but yesterday, and every day I live it sinks deeper into my heart."

[3] A scrivener is a broker and money-lender.

LIFE OF GRAY.

ber 26,⁴ 1716. His grammatical education he received at Eton,⁵ under the care of Mr. Antrobus, his mother's brother, then assistant to Dr. George; and when he left school, in 1734, entered a pensioner at Peterhouse, in Cambridge.⁶

The transition from the school to the college is, to most young scholars, the time from which they date their years of manhood, liberty, and happiness; but Gray seems to have been very little delighted with academical gratifications; he liked at Cambridge neither the mode of life nor the fashion of study, and lived sullenly on to the time when his attendance on lectures was no longer required. As he intended to profess the common law, he took no degree.

When he had been at Cambridge about five years,⁷ Mr. Horace Walpole, whose friendship he had gained at Eton, invited him to travel with him as his companion. They wandered through France into Italy; and Gray's Letters contain a very pleasing account of many parts of their journey. But unequal friendships are easily dissolved: at Florence⁸ they quarrelled, and parted; and Mr. Walpole is now content to have it told that it was by his fault. If we look, however, without prejudice on the

---

⁴ Read December 26.

⁵ Of his school-life we know very little. His uncle, Horace Walpole tells us, "Took prodigious pains with him, which answered exceedingly." He was a shy, retiring boy, with no turn for games, and used to read Vergil in play-hours for his own amusement.

⁶ His Eton uncle selected Peterhouse, being himself a fellow of the College. "The studies of the place were mathematics, the recreation was drinking, and he had no taste for either. Classical learning, which had been everything at Eton, he found was held in disdain; and after submitting with aversion to a formal attendance on the usual routine of lectures, he came to the determination not to take a degree."—*Quarterly Review*.

⁷ He left Cambridge in September, 1738, and for the next six months lived with his father and mother in London.

⁸ It was at Reggio. The causes of the quarrel are not far to seek. Walpole was all for society and gaieties; Gray cared for nothing but antiquities, art, and scenery. Walpole was patronizing, and Gray was sensitive to a fault. It is said on fair authority that the final breach was caused by Gray's discovering

The leading
Works of Milton
 Poems
Ode on the Nativity
L'Allegro, Il Penseroso
Arcades, Comus
Lycidas Paradise lost
Paradise Regained
 Prose Works
Areopagitica,
The Tenure of Kings
Eikonoklastes

f Indolence
el Richards
a. Clarissa
*Charles Gran**d*
ry Fielding, J
rews, Jonath
lia

s Smollett,
ick Nandon
mphrey - Cli
d Hume, A
n Nature. His
d

ene Robertso
y of Scotland, h

world, we shall find that men, whose consciousness of their own merit sets them above the compliances of servility, are apt enough in their association with superiors to watch their own dignity with troublesome and punctilious jealousy, and in the fervour of independence to exact that attention which they refuse to pay. Part they did, whatever was the quarrel; and the rest of their travels was doubtless more unpleasant to them both. Gray continued his journey in a manner suitable to his own little fortune, with only an occasional servant.

He returned to England in September, 1741, and in about two months afterwards buried his father, who had, by an injudicious waste of money upon a new house, so much lessened his fortune that Gray thought himself too poor to study the law. He therefore retired to Cambridge, where he soon after became Bachelor of Civil Law, and where, without liking the place or its inhabitants, or professing to like them, he passed, except a short residence at London, the rest of his life.

About this time he was deprived of Mr. West,[9] the son of a chancellor of Ireland, a friend on whom he appears to have set a high value, and who deserved his esteem by the powers which he shows in his Letters, and in the *Ode to May*, which Mr. Mason has preserved, as well as by the sincerity with which, when Gray sent him part of *Agrippina*, a tragedy that he had just begun, he gave an opinion which probably intercepted the progress of the work, and which the judgment of every reader will confirm. It was certainly no loss to the English stage that *Agrippina* was never finished.

In this year (1742) Gray seems to have applied himself seriously to poetry; for in this year were produced the *Ode to Spring*, his *Prospect of Eton*, and his *Ode to Adversity*. He began likewise a Latin poem, *De principiis cogitandi*.[10]

It may be collected from the narrative of Mr. Mason,

---

that Walpole had opened one of his letters. Walpole was quite capable of such a meanness; and though many years after a partial reconciliation took place, the fault, whatever it may have been, was never forgiven by Gray.

[9] See note to sonnet on Richard West.

[10] The English title might run, 'On the five gateways of knowledge.' For a specimen see note, page 83.

that his first ambition was to have excelled in Latin poetry; perhaps it were reasonable to wish that he had prosecuted his design; for, though there is at present some embarrassment in his phrase, and some harshness in his lyric numbers, his copiousness of language is such as very few possess; and his lines, even when imperfect, discover a writer whom practice would have made skilful.[11]

He now lived on at Peterhouse, very little solicitous what others did or thought, and cultivated his mind and enlarged his views without any other purpose than of improving and amusing himself; when Mr. Mason,[12] being elected Fellow of Pembroke Hall, brought him a companion who was afterwards to be his editor, and whose fondness and fidelity has kindled in him a zeal of admiration which cannot be reasonably expected from the neutrality of a stranger, and the coldness of a critic.

In this retirement he wrote (1747) an ode on the *Death of Mr. Walpole's Cat;* and the year afterwards attempted a poem, of more importance, on *Government and Education*,[13] of which the fragments which remain have many excellent lines. His next production (1750) was his far-famed *Elegy in the Churchyard*, which, finding its way into a magazine, first, I believe, made him known to the public.[14]

---

[11] Johnson's wish is father to the thought that Gray is but a second-rate English poet. No poet has ever written verses in a foreign tongue which have obtained more than a *succès d'estime*. Who now reads even Milton or Petrarch's Latin poems, except as literary curiosities?

[12] The Rev. William Mason (1725-1797), a third-rate poet, was the friend and literary executor of Gray. His character for literary fidelity received a rude shock by the publication of the works of Thomas Gray by the Rev. John Mitford, 1837-1843. Mitford has shown that Mason deliberately altered, interpolated, and jumbled together Gray's correspondence, and, what was worse, destroyed the originals with which he had taken these unwarrantable liberties.

[13] This fragment has not been included in this edition. It has all the faults of a didactic, philosophic poem, such as Pope's *Essay on Man*, and none of the knowledge of the world, the brilliant wit and happy illustration, which make us still read the *Essay* in spite of its philosophy.

[14] In February, 1751, Gray received a letter from the editor of the *Magazine of Magazines*, informing him that his "ingenious

Samuel Johnson, Rasselas, Rambler, London, A Life of Savage, The Vanity of Human Wishes, Diction of English Language

Edward Gibbon, The Decline and Fall of the Roman Empire

Robert Burns, To a Daisy, an a Mouse, The Cottar's Saturday Night, Elegy on Captain Mathew Henderson, Tam O'Shanter

Edmund Burke, The Vindication of Natural Society, Essay on the Sublime and Beautiful

Lord Byron, Childe Harold's Pilgrimage, Corsair, Lara

George Crabbe, The Village, The Library, The Parish Register

Walter Scott, Waverley, The Lay of The Last Minstrel, Marmion, Lady of the Lake, Rob Roy, The Lord of the Isles, Woodstock, Rokeby, Vision of Don Roderick

An invitation from Lady Cobham about this time gave occasion to an odd composition called *A Long Story*,[15] which adds little to Gray's character.

Several of his pieces were published (1753), with designs by Mr. Bentley; and, that they might in some form or other make a book, only one side of each leaf was printed. I believe the poems and the plates recommended each other so well, that the whole impression was soon bought. This year he lost his mother.

Some time afterwards (1756) some young men of the college, whose chambers were near his, diverted themselves with disturbing him by frequent and troublesome noises, and, as is said, by pranks yet more offensive and contemptuous.[16] This insolence, having endured it awhile, he represented to the governors of the society, among whom perhaps he had no friends; and, finding his complaint little regarded, removed himself to Pembroke Hall.

In 1759 he published *The Progress of Poetry* and *The Bard*, two compositions at which the readers of poetry were at first content to gaze in mute amazement.[17] Some that tried them confessed their inability to understand them, though Warburton said that they were understood as well as the works of Milton and Shakespeare, which it is the fashion to admire. Garrick wrote a few lines in

---

poem" was in the press. In order to forestall the magazine, Gray wrote to Walpole to beg him to negotiate with Dodsley, and get him to print the elegy at once without a name.

[15] Lady Cobham, who lived at the Mansion House at Stoke-Pogeis, near Windsor, wished to make the acquaintance of her neighbour the poet, who was at that time living with his aunt. Two ladies, who were staying with Lady Cobham, volunteered to call upon him, and finding him out left their cards. Gray soon became intimate with the ladies, and wrote the poem giving a humorous account of the visit. Gray had nothing of the playful humour and lightness of touch which *vers de société* demand, and I have not cared to disinter these verses, which Gray himself would never allow to be reprinted.

[16] Gray, who was afraid of fire, had procured himself a laddei of ropes. The opportunity for a practical joke was too good to be lost, and some of the Peterhouse undergraduates raised at midnight a cry of fire in the hopes of seeing the poet descend.

[17] Goldsmith among the number: "They have caught the seeming obscurity of Pindar;" "They can at best amuse only the few," and so on.—In *Monthly Review*.

their praise. Some hardy champions[18] undertook to rescue them from neglect; and in a short time many were content to be shown beauties which they could not see.

Gray's reputation was now so high, that, after the death of Cibber, he had the honour of refusing the laurel, which was then bestowed on Mr. Whitehead.[19]

His curiosity, not long after, drew him away from Cambridge to a lodging near the Museum,[20] where he resided near three years, reading and transcribing; and, so far as can be discovered, very little affected by two odes on *Oblivion* and *Obscurity*,[21] in which his lyric performances were ridiculed with much contempt and much ingenuity.

When the Professor of Modern History at Cambridge died, he was, as he says, "cockered and spirited up," till he asked it of Lord Bute, who sent him a civil refusal; and the place was given to Mr. Brocket, the tutor of Sir James Lowther.

His constitution was weak, and, believing that his health was promoted by exercise and change of place, he undertook (1765) a journey into Scotland, of which his account, so far as it extends, is very curious and elegant: for, as his comprehension was ample, his curiosity extended to all the works of art, all the appearances of nature, and all

---

[18] Wharton and Mason in chief.

[19] Colley Cibber, Poet Laureate, 1730-1757; W. Whitehead, Poet Laureate, 1757-1785. *Arcades ambo!* See Appendix, Letter xii.

[20] In 1753 lotteries were started to purchase the Sloane collection and the Harleian MSS., which were combined with the Cottonian collection, and deposited in Montague House, under the name of the British Museum. (Lecky, *History of England in XVIIIth Century*, vol. i. p. 523.) It was opened to the public in 1759, and in the July of that year Gray took lodgings in Southampton Row, in order to study and transcribe the historical and genealogical MSS. He gives in his letter an amusing account of the reading-room, where he regularly passed four hours a day. There were but five occupants—two Prussians; a third gentleman who wrote for Lord Royston; "Dr. Stukeley, who writes for himself, the very worst person he could write for; and I, who only read to know if there is anything worth writing." The present reading-room, opened 1857, accommodates three hundred readers, and is generally full.

[21] By Colman and Lloyd. *Oblivion* was a parody of Mason, not Gray.

"People of one country are as happy as another" Twenty Plazzie, words using contrast

John Keats, Hyperion
Thalaba the Destroyer by D. John Southey
Ancient Mariner by Coleridge
The Excursion W Wordsworth

Charles Dickens,
Pickwick Papers, The
Morning Chronicle
Nicholas Nickleby

William Makepeace Thackeray
Vanity Fair, The Snobs of
England, The History of
Pendennis, The History of
Henry Esmond, The town
Georges

the monuments of past events. He naturally contracted a friendship with Dr. Beattie,[22] whom he found a poet, a philosopher, and a good man. The Mareschal College at Aberdeen offered him a degree of Doctor of Laws, which, having omitted to take it at Cambridge, he thought it decent to refuse.

What he had formerly solicited in vain was at last given him without solicitation. The professorship of history became again vacant, and he received (1768) an offer of it from the Duke of Grafton. He accepted, and retained it to his death; always designing lectures, but never reading them; uneasy at his neglect of duty, and appeasing his uneasiness with designs of reformation, and with a resolution which he believed himself to have made of resigning the office, if he found himself unable to discharge it.

Ill health made another journey necessary, and he visited (1769) Westmoreland and Cumberland. He that reads his epistolary narration wishes, that to travel, and to tell his travels, had been more of his employment; but it is by studying at home that we must obtain the ability of travelling with intelligence and improvement.

His travels and his studies were now near their end. The gout, of which he had sustained many weak attacks, fell upon his stomach, and, yielding to no medicines, produced strong convulsions, which (July 30th, 1771) terminated in death.[23] His character I am willing to adopt, as Mr. Mason has done, from a letter written to my friend Mr. Boswell, by the Rev. Mr. Temple, rector of St. Gluvias in Cornwall; and am as willing as his warmest well-wisher to believe it true.

"Perhaps he was the most learned man in Europe. He was equally acquainted with the elegant and profound parts of science, and that not superficially, but thoroughly. He knew every branch of history, both natural and civil; had read all the original historians of England, France, and Italy; and was a great antiquarian. Criticism, metaphysics, morals, politics, made a principal part of his study; voyages and travels of all sorts were his favourite

---

[22] James Beattie (1735-1802); best known by his poem, *The Minstrel*, written in the stanza and manner of Spenser.

[23] He died at Pembroke Hall, and was buried by his own desire beside his mother in the churchyard of Stoke-Pogeis.

amusements; and he had a fine taste in painting, prints, architecture, and gardening. With such a fund of knowledge, his conversation must have been equally instructing and entertaining; but he was also a good man, a man of virtue and humanity. There is no character without some speck, some imperfection; and I think the greatest defect in his was an affectation in delicacy, or rather effeminacy, and a visible fastidiousness, or contempt and disdain of his inferiors in science. He also had, in some degree, that weakness which disgusted Voltaire so much in Mr. Congreve:[24] though he seemed to value others chiefly according to the progress they had made in knowledge, yet he could not bear to be considered merely as a man of letters; and, though without birth, or fortune, or station, his desire was to be looked upon as a private independent gentleman, who read for his amusement. Perhaps it may be said, What signifies so much knowledge, when it produced so little? Is it worth taking so much pains to leave no memorial but a few poems? But let it be considered that Mr. Gray was to others at least innocently employed; to himself certainly beneficially. His time passed agreeably: he was every day making some new acquisition in science; his mind was enlarged, his heart softened, his virtue strengthened; the world and mankind were shown to him without a mask; and he was taught to consider everything as trifling, and unworthy of the attention of a wise man, except the pursuit of knowledge and practice of virtue in that state wherein God hath placed us."

To this character Mr. Mason has added a more particular account of Gray's skill in zoology. He has remarked that Gray's effeminacy was affected most "before those whom he did not wish to please;" and that he is unjustly charged with making knowledge his sole reason of preference, as he paid his esteem to none whom he did not likewise believe to be good.

---

[24] The affectation of the airs of a fine gentleman. "But he treated the Muses with ingratitude; for, having long conversed familiarly with the great, he wished to be considered rather as a man of fashion and wit; and when he received a visit from Voltaire disgusted him by the despicable foppery of desiring to be considered not as an author, but a gentleman, to which the Frenchman replied, 'that if he had been only a gentleman he should not have come to visit him.'"—Johnson's *Life of Congreve.*

/

Give an outline of Cromwell's life and character

Mention the muses with the province of literature assigned to each

Is the epitaph a correct delineation of the character of the person for whom it was intended?

LIFE OF GRAY.

What has occurred to me from the slight inspection of his letters in which my undertaking has engaged me is, that his mind had a large grasp ; that his curiosity was unlimited, and his judgment cultivated ; that he was a man likely to love much where he loved at all; but that he was fastidious and hard to please. His contempt, however, is often employed, where I hope it will be approved, upon scepticism and infidelity. His short account of Shaftesbury[25] I will insert.

"You say you cannot conceive how Lord Shaftesbury came to be a philosopher in vogue ; I will tell you : first, he was a lord ; secondly, he was as vain as any of his readers ; thirdly, men are very prone to believe what they do not understand ; fourthly, they will believe anything at all, provided they are under no obligation to believe it ; fifthly, they love to take a new road, even when that road leads nowhere ; sixthly, he was reckoned a fine writer, and seems always to mean more than he said. Would you have any more reasons? An interval of about forty years has pretty well destroyed the charm. A dead lord ranks with commoners ; vanity is no longer interested in the matter ; for a new road has become an old one."

Mr. Mason has added, from his own knowledge, that, though Gray was poor, he was not eager of money ; and that, out of the little that he had, he was very willing to help the necessitous.

As a writer he had this peculiarity, that he did not write his pieces first rudely, and then correct them, but laboured every line as it arose in the train of composition ; and he had a notion not very peculiar, that he could not write but at certain times, or at happy moments ; a fantastic foppery, to which my kindness for a man of learning and virtue wishes him to have been superior.[26]

---

[25] Shaftesbury (1671–1713), the moralist and metaphysician. His collected works bear the title of *Characteristics*. On Gray's letters, the judgment of Cowper, himself pre-eminent as a letter-writer, is worth quoting : "I have been reading Gray's works, and think him sublime. . . . I once thought Swift's letters the best that could be written, but I like Gray's better. His humour, or his wit, or whatever it is to be called, is never illnatured or offensive, and yet I think equally poignant with the Dean's."

[26] "I by no means pretend to inspiration, but yet I affirm that the faculty in question is by no means voluntary. It is the

Gray's poetry is now to be considered; and I hope not to be looked on as an enemy to his name, if I confess that I contemplate it with less pleasure than his life. His ode *On Spring* has something poetical, both in the language and the thought; but the language is too luxuriant, and the thoughts have nothing new. There has of late arisen a practice of giving to adjectives derived from substantives the termination of participles; such as the *cultured* plain, the *daisied* bank; but I was sorry to see, in the lines of a scholar like Gray, the *honied* Spring.[27] The morality is natural, but too stale; the conclusion is pretty.

The poem *On the Cat* was doubtless by its author considered as a trifle, but it is not a happy trifle. In the first stanza, "the azure flowers *that blow*" show how resolutely a rhyme is sometimes made when it cannot easily be found. Selima, the cat, is called a nymph, with some violence both to language and sense; but there is no good use made of it when it is done; for of the two lines,

What female heart can gold despise?
What cat's averse to fish?

the first relates merely to the nymph, and the second only to the cat. The sixth stanza contains a melancholy truth, that "a favourite has no friend;" but the last ends in a pointed sentence of no relation to the purpose; if *what glistered* had been *gold*, the cat would not have gone

---

result I suppose of a certain disposition of mind, which does not depend on one's self, and which I have not felt this long time. You that are a witness how seldom this spirit has moved me in my life, may easily give credit to what I say." (GRAY to Dr. Wharton, 1758.) Compare Johnson's observations on the tradition preserved by Philips, that Milton's vein never happily flowed but from the autumnal equinox to the vernal. "The dependence of the soul upon the seasons, those temporary and periodical ebbs and flows of the intellect, may, I suppose, justly be derided as the fumes of vain imagination." Such opposite natures as Gray and Johnson, the fastidious dilettante and the robust dictionary maker, were not likely to understand one another.

[27] This captious bit of criticism hardly needs refutation. "Honied" is in Shakespeare and Milton. Turning to Johnson's own poems, I find near the beginning of *London* "a titled poet." Such adjectives formed from substantives are quite in keeping with the genius of the English language.

Give the substance of the
criticisms of the Elegy published
in the monthly review?

Give an acc of Milton and
His Works.

Paradise Lost
    "   Regained

Who were the parliamen-
tary Orators about the
time of the E, Pitt, Walpole,
Burke, Grenville.

What was the state of Education
among the masses in Gray's time

into the water; and, if she had, would not less have been drowned.

The Prospect of Eton College, suggests nothing to Gray which every beholder does not equally think and feel. His supplication to Father Thames,[28] to tell him who drives the hoop or tosses the ball, is useless and puerile. Father Thames has no better means of knowing than himself. His epithet "buxom health"[29] is not elegant; he seems not to understand the word. Gray thought his language more poetical as it was more remote from common use: finding in Dryden "honey redolent of spring,"[30] an expression that reaches the utmost limits of our language, Gray drove it a little more beyond common apprehension, by making "gales" to be "redolent of joy and youth."

Of the *Ode on Adversity*, the hint was at first taken from "*O Diva, gratum quæ regis Antium;*" but Gray has excelled his original by the variety of his sentiments, and by their moral application. Of this piece, at once poetical and rational, I will not by slight objections violate the dignity.

My process has now brought me to the *wonderful Wonder of Wonders*, the two sister odes, by which, though either vulgar ignorance or common sense at first universally rejected them, many have been since persuaded to think themselves delighted. I am one of those that are willing to be pleased, and therefore would gladly find the meaning of the first stanza of the *Progress of Poetry*. Gray seems in his rapture to confound the images of spreading sound and running water. A "stream of music" may be allowed; but where does "music," however "smooth and strong," after having visited the " verdant vales, roll down the steep amain," so as that "rocks and nodding groves rebellow to the roar"? If this be said of music,

---

[28] Lord Grenville has most happily hoist the enginer with his own petar: "He forgets his own address to the Nile in Rasselas for a purpose so very similar, and he forgets his readers to forget one of the most affecting passages in Virgil. Father Thames might well know as much of the sports of boys as the 'great Father of Waters' knew of the discontents of men, or the Tiber himself of the obsequies of Marcellus."

[29] See note on line 45.
[30] See note on line 19.

it is nonsense; if it be said of water, it is nothing to the purpose.

The second stanza, exhibiting Mars' car and Jove's eagle, is unworthy of further notice. Criticism disdains to chase a schoolboy to his common-places.[31]

To the third it may likewise be objected, that it is drawn from mythology, though such as may be more easily assimilated to real life. Idalia's "velvet green" has something of cant. An epithet or metaphor drawn from Nature ennobles Art; an epithet or metaphor drawn from Art degrades Nature.[32] Gray is too fond of words arbitrarily compounded. "Many-twinkling" was formerly censured as not analogical; we may say "many-spotted;" but scarcely "many-spotting." This stanza, however, has something pleasing.

Of the second ternary of stanzas, the first endeavours to tell something, and would have told it, had it not been crossed by Hyperion; the second describes well enough the universal prevalence of poetry; but I am afraid that the conclusion will not rise from the premises. The caverns of the North, and the plains of Chili, are not the residences of "glory and generous shame." But that poetry and virtue go always together is an opinion so pleasing, that I can forgive him who resolves to think it true.

---

[31] "That the 'Phoebus' is hacknied," says Coleridge, speaking of another of Gray's poems, "and a schoolboy image, is an accidental fault, dependent on the age in which the author wrote, and not deduced from the nature of the thing. That it is part of an exploded mythology is an objection more deeply grounded. Yet when the torch of ancient learning was rekindled, so cheering were its beams, that our eldest poets, cut off by Christianity from all accredited machinery, and deprived of all acknowledged guardians and symbols of the great objects of nature, were naturally induced to adopt as a poetic language those fabulous personages, those forms of the supernatural in nature, which had given them such dear delight in the poems of their great masters. Nay, even at this day, what scholar of genial taste will not so far sympathize with them as to read with pleasure in Petrarch, Chaucer, or Spenser what he would perhaps condemn as puerile in a modern poet?"

[32] Another untenable canon of criticism, disproved by endless examples, from the Psalmist's "He giveth His snow like wool," to Tennyson's "Slow-dropping veils of thinnest lawn." Look at Milton's *Lycidas* for illustration.

Give a chronological list of Gray's works.

"Ode to Spring" 1742
" " " Eaton College" 1742
"Hymn to Adversity" 1742
"Elegy in a country churchyard" 1750
"Progress of Poetry" ~~1754~~ 1757
"The Bard" 1757

Give a History of H. Curfew and state the ~~last~~ meaning of the word in line I

Sketch the history of the
production of the Elegy

How many editions
of E. were published in
G's lifetime

Into what Languages has
it been translated

Sketch the part taken by
Hampden in the defence of
Liberty

What reasons have been given
for Johnson's contempt of Gray's
productions?

Point out every allusion to
events of the time and
condition of the people

The third stanza sounds big with "Delphi," and "Egean," and "Ilissus," and "Meander," and "hallowed fountains," and "solemn sound;" but in all Gray's odes there is a kind of cumbrous splendour which we wish away. His position is at last false. In the time of Dante and Petrarch, from whom we derive our first school of poetry, Italy was overrun by "tyrant power" and "coward vice;" nor was our state much better when we first borrowed the Italian arts.

Of the third ternary, the first gives a mythological birth of Shakespeare. What is said of that mighty genius is true, but it is not said happily; the real effects of this poetical power are put out of sight by the pomp of machinery. Where truth is sufficient to fill the mind, fiction is worse than useless; the counterfeit debases the genuine.

His account of Milton's blindness, if we suppose it caused by study in the formation of his poem, a supposition surely allowable, is poetically true, and happily imagined. But the *car* of Dryden, with his *two coursers*, has nothing in it peculiar; it is a car in which any other rider may be placed.

The Bard appears, at the first view, to be, as Algarotti[33] and others have remarked, an imitation of the prophecy of Nereus. Algarotti thinks it superior to its original; and, if preference depends only on the imagery and animation of the two poems, his judgment is right. There is in *The Bard* more force, more thought, and more variety. But to copy is less than to invent, and the copy has been unhappily produced at a wrong time. The fiction of Horace was to the Romans credible; but its revival disgusts us with apparent and unconquerable falsehood. *Incredulus odi.*[34]

To select a singular event, and swell it to a giant's bulk

---

[33] Count Algarotti (1712–1764), a Venetian by birth, a distinguished littérateur, art-critic, and popularizer of science. A common triend, Mr. Howe, introduced him to Gray's poems, which he greatly admired, and this led to a correspondence between him and Gray.

[34] From Horace, *Ars Poetica*, 188:
    Quodcunque ostendis mihi sic incredulus odi.
(Of the metamorphoses of Progne into a bird, Cadmus into a snake, &c.)

by fabulous appendages of spectres and predictions, has little difficulty; for he that forsakes the probable may always find the marvellous. And it has little use; we are affected only as we believe; we are improved only as we find something to be imitated or declined. I do not see that *The Bard* promotes any truth, moral or political.[35]

His stanzas are too long, especially his epodes; the ode is finished before the ear has learned its measures, and consequently before it can receive pleasure from their consonance and recurrence.

Of the first stanza the abrupt beginning has been celebrated; but technical beauties can give praise only to the inventor. It is in the power of any man to rush abruptly upon his subject that has read the ballad of *Johnny Armstrong*,[36]

Is there ever a man in all Scotland—

The initial resemblances or alliterations, "ruin, ruthless," "helm or hauberk," are below the grandeur of a poem that endeavours at sublimity.

In the second stanza the Bard is well described; but in the third we have the puerilities of obsolete mythology. When we are told that "Cadwallo hush'd the stormy main," and that "Modred made huge Plinlimmon bow his cloud-topp'd head," attention recoils from the repetition of a tale that, even when it was first heard, was heard with scorn.

The *weaving* of the *winding-sheet* he borrowed, as he owns, from the Northern Bards; but their texture, however, was very properly the work of female powers, as the act of spinning the thread of life in another mythology. Theft is always dangerous; Gray has made weavers of slaughtered bards by a fiction outrageous and incongruous. They are then called upon to "Weave the warp, and weave the woof," perhaps with no great propriety; for it is by crossing the *woof* with the *warp* that men weave

---

[35] We are reminded of the Scotchman who, after reading *Paradise Lost*, wanted to know what it proved.

[36] Is there ever a man in all Scotland,
 From the highest estate to the lowest degree,
 That can show himself now before our King—
 Scotland's so full of treacherie?

The best version is in *Wit Restor'd* (1658).

Compare the power of
description of G. & Gold?
illustrating by passage
from the L. + E.
Goldsmith described from nature
Gray described from fancy
Gold. is careless
Gray is fistidious
what are the characteristics of
G. poetical and Prose
writings? They are all very
carefully written. They display
Scholarship, Genius

Whom did Gray profess to
adopt as his model.
 Dryden

egy. is a mournful Poem
Epitaph is written on a tombstone
Dirge is a Funeral hymn

The E. first appeared with
Magazine of Magazines
It was begun in 1742, and was
finished in 1750

Quote Dr Johnsons opinion
of the E. and criticise it.
Abounds with images
which find a mirror in
every mind and with
sentiments which every
bosom returns an echo
In the character of the Elegy
I rejoice to concur with the
common Reader. I ...

the *web* or piece ; and the first line was dearly bought by the admission of its wretched correspondent, "Give ample room and verge enough." He has, however, no other line as bad.

The third stanza of the second ternary is commended, I think, beyond its merit. The personification is indistinct. *Thirst* and *hunger* are not alike; and their features, to make the imagery perfect, should have been discriminated. We are told in the same stanza how "towers are fed." But I will no longer look for particular faults; yet let it be observed that the ode might have been concluded with an action of better example; but suicide is always to be had, without expense of thought.

These odes are marked by glittering accumulations of ungraceful ornaments; they strike rather than please; the images are magnified by affectation; the language is laboured into harshness. The mind of the writer seems to work with unnatural violence. "Double, double, toil and trouble." He has a kind of strutting dignity, and is tall by walking on tiptoe. His art and his struggle are too visible, and there is too little appearance of ease and nature.

To say that he has no beauties would be unjust: a man like him, of great learning and great industry, could not but produce something valuable. When he pleases least, it can only be said that a good design was ill directed.

His translations of Northern and Welsh poetry deserve praise; the imagery is preserved, perhaps often improved; but the language is unlike the language of other poets.

In the character of his *Elegy* I rejoice to concur with the common reader; for by the common sense of readers, uncorrupted with literary prejudices, after all the refinements of subtilty and the dogmatism of learning, must be finally decided all claim to poetical honours. The *Churchyard* abounds with images which find a mirror in every mind, and with sentiments to which every bosom returns an echo. The four stanzas beginning, "Yet even these bones," are to me original: I have never seen the notions in any other place; yet he that reads them here persuades himself that he has always felt them. Had Gray written often thus, it had been vain to blame, and useless to praise him.

SELECTIONS FROM GRAY'S LETTERS

MR. GRAY TO MR. WALPOLE.
CAMBRIDGE, *Feb.* 11, 1751.

As you have brought me into a little sort of distress, you must assist me, I believe, to get out of it as well as I can. Yesterday I had the misfortune of receiving a letter from certain gentlemen (as their bookseller expresses it), who have taken the *Magazine of Magazines* into their hands: They tell me that an *ingenious* Poem, called reflections in a Country Church-yard, has been communicated to them, which they are printing forthwith; that they are informed that the *excellent* author of it is I by name, and that they beg not only his *indulgence*, but the *honour* of his correspondence, &c. As I am not at all disposed to be either so indulgent, or so correspondent, as they desire, I have but one bad way left to escape the honour they would inflict upon me; and therefore am obliged to desire you would make Dodsley print it immediately (which may be done in less than a week's time) from your copy, but without my name, in what form is most convenient for him, but on his best paper and character; he must correct the press himself, and print it without any interval between the stanzas, because the sense is in some places continued beyond them; and the title must be,—Elegy, written in a Country Church-yard. If he would add a line or two to say it came into his hands by accident, I should like it better. If you behold the *Magazine of Magazines* in the light that I do, you will not refuse to give yourself this trouble on my account, which you have taken of your own accord before now. If Dodsley do not do this immediately, he may as well let it alone.

NOTE.—Gray succeeded in forestalling the magazines by a few days. The first edition, as is proved by the next letter, was out by February 20. Its title ran, "*An Elegy wrote in a Country Church-yard.* London: Printed for R. Dodsley in Pall Mall, and sold by M. Cooper in Paternoster Row, 1751. Price 6d." It appeared in the *Magazine of Magazines* for February, in the *London Magazine* for March, and in the *Grand Magazine of Magazines* for April, 1751. Magazines at that period came out at the end of the month.

The peculiar charm of the Elegy is because it appeals to the feelings of all mankind & its melody

"Immortality of the soul" by Davies

"Annus Mirabilis the wonderfull year" Dryden these were written prove the elegy is sense quo tram-

What is an Elegy.

Make a list of elegiac poems with authors
Elegy of Churchyard, Gray
Tennyson's in memoriam
Milton's Lycidas
dirago dirago
from, dirage dress in mors words of Latin/Hym

The reason of The Elegy being so popular is because it means all Mankind

Elegy means? A Mournful Song
              Derivation of Elegy
Elegy { e l Legia } (Algos, Pain)
  "   { (Eleleu meaning alas) }

(1) The Churchyard was Stoke Pogis
(2) "   "   "   " (Burnham Beeches)
(3) "   "   "   " (Grenchester)
(4) "   "   "   " (Mardingly)

Glimmer is frequentative of Gleam

Molest and pry into her ancient reign, is another reading for (12)

London Scotland Wales 1746-1771

ELEGY

WRITTEN IN A COUNTRY CHURCHYARD.

THE curfew tolls the knell of parting day,
The lowing herd wind slowly o'er the lea,
The ploughman homeward plods his weary way,
And leaves the world to darkness and to me.

Now fades the glimmering landscape on the sight, 5
And all the air a solemn stillness holds,
Save where the beetle wheels his droning flight,
And drowsy tinklings lull the distant folds;

Save that from yonder ivy-mantled tower,
The moping owl does to the moon complain 10
Of such as wand'ring near her secret bower,
Molest her ancient solitary reign.

Beneath those rugged elms, that yew-tree's shade,
Where heaves the turf in many a mould'ring heap,
Each in his narrow cell for ever laid, 15
The rude Forefathers of the hamlet sleep.

The breezy call of incense-breathing Morn,
The swallow twitt'ring from the straw-built shed,
The cock's shrill clarion, or the echoing horn,
No more shall rouse them from their lowly bed. 20

For them no more the blazing hearth shall burn,
Or busy housewife ply her evening care:
No children run to lisp their sire's return,
Or climb his knees the envied kiss to share.

Oft did the harvest to their sickle yield, 25
Their furrow oft the stubborn glebe has broke;
How jocund did they drive their team afield!
How bow'd the woods beneath their sturdy stroke!

Let not Ambition mock their useful toil,
Their homely joys, and destiny obscure;
Nor Grandeur hear with a disdainful smile,
The short and simple annals of the Poor.

The boast of heraldry, the pomp of power,
And all that beauty, all that wealth e'er gave,
Awaits alike the inevitable hour.
The paths of glory lead but to the grave.

Nor you, ye Proud, impute to these the fault,
If Memory o'er their tomb no trophies raise,
Where through the long-drawn aisle and fretted vault
The pealing anthem swells the note of praise.   40

Can storied urn or animated bust
Back to its mansion call the fleeting breath?
Can Honour's voice provoke the silent dust,
Or Flattery soothe the dull cold ear of Death?

Perhaps in this neglected spot is laid   45
Some heart once pregnant with celestial fire;
Hands, that the rod of empire might have sway'd,
Or wak'd to ecstasy the living lyre.

But Knowledge to their eyes her ample page,
Rich with the spoils of time, did ne'er unroll;   50
Chill Penury repress'd their noble rage,
And froze the genial current of the soul.

Full many a gem of purest ray serene,
The dark unfathomed caves of ocean bear;
Full many a flower is born to blush unseen,   55
And waste its sweetness on the desert air.

Some village-Hampden, that with dauntless breast
The little tyrant of his fields withstood;
Some mute inglorious Milton here may rest,
Some Cromwell guiltless of his country's blood.   60

Th' applause of list'ning senates to command,
The threats of pain and ruin to despise,
To scatter plenty o'er a smiling land,
And read their history in a nation's eyes,

ELEGY.

Their lot forbade : nor circumscrib'd alone 65
Their growing virtues, but their crimes confin'd ;
Forbad to wade through slaughter to a throne,
And shut the gates of mercy on mankind,

The struggling pangs of conscious truth to hide,
To quench the blushes of ingenuous shame, 70
Or heap the shrine of Luxury and Pride
With incense kindled at the Muse's flame.

Far from the madding crowd's ignoble strife,
Their sober wishes never learned to stray ;
Along the cool sequester'd vale of life 75
They kept the noiseless tenor of their way.

Yet e'en these bones from insult to protect
Some frail memorial still erected nigh,
With uncouth rhimes and shapeless sculpture deck'd,
Implores the passing tribute of a sigh, 80

Their name, their years, spelt by th' unlettered muse,
The place of fame and elegy supply :
And many a holy text around she strews,
That teach the rustic moralist to die.

For who to dumb Forgetfulness a prey, 85
This pleasing anxious being e'er resign'd,
Left the warm precincts of the cheerful day,
Nor cast one longing, lingering look behind?

On some fond breast the parting soul relies,
Some pious drops the closing eye requires ; 90
E'en from the tomb the voice of Nature cries,
E'en in our ashes live their wonted fires.

For thee, who, mindful of th' unhonour'd dead,
Dost in these lines their artless tale relate ;
If chance, by lonely contemplation led, 95
Some kindred spirit shall inquire thy fate.

Haply some hoary-headed swain may say :
"Oft have we seen him at the peep of dawn
Brushing with hasty step the dews away
To meet the sun upon the upland lawn. 100

"There at the foot of yonder nodding beech
That wreathes its old fantastic roots so high,
His listless length at noontide would he stretch,
And pore upon the brook that babbles by.

"Hard by yon wood, now smiling as in scorn,   105
Mutt'ring his wayward fancies he would rove;
Now drooping, woful wan, like one forlorn,
Or craz'd with care, or cross'd in hopeless love.

"One morn I miss'd him on the customed hill,
Along the heath and near his favourite tree;   110
Another came; nor yet beside the rill,
Nor up the lawn, nor at the wood was he;

"The next with dirges due in sad array
Slow through the church-way path we saw him borne.
Approach and read (for thou can'st read) the lay,   115
Grav'd on the stone beneath yon aged thorn."

THE EPITAPH.

HERE rests his head upon the lap of Earth,
A Youth to Fortune and to Fame unknown;
Fair Science frown'd not on his humble birth,
And Melancholy marked him for her own.   120

Large was his bounty, and his soul sincere,
Heaven did a recompense as largely send;
He gave to Misery all he had—a tear,
He gained from heaven ('twas all he wished) a friend.

No farther seek his merits to disclose,   125
Or draw his frailties from their dread abode
(There they alike in trembling hope repose),
The bosom of his Father and his God.

The Elegy is an Iambic
Pentameter, and an
Elegiac Heroics

NOTES

THE ELEGY.

1 *Curfew.* Used by Bacon in the literal sense of a fire-cover, a grate. The time for the curfew bell varied from three to eight. Cf. Shakespeare's *Romeo and Juliet*, act iv. scene 4, l. 4—
". . . "The second cock hath crow'd,
The curfew bell hath rung, 't is three o'clock."
Gray quotes Dante, *Purgatorio*, 8—
"Squilla di lontano
Che paia 'l giorno pianger, che si muore."
("Hears the vesper bell from far,
That seems to mourn for the expiring day.")
Parting. 'Departing.' Prefixes are constantly dropped in Elizabethan English—'braid for upbraid, 'file for defile, 'collect for recollect. *Dying* of the first draft was changed to *parting*, to avoid the conceit. It is said that Gray had originally inserted a comma after "tolls," but the printer omitted it, and Gray adopted the emendation.

2 *Lea.* Meadow-land or forest glade, where the cattle love to *lie*. Common both as a prefix and suffix in names of places—Leighton, Hadleigh, Brenchley, &c.

4 Cf. Petrarch—
"Quando 'l sol bagna in mar l'aurato cerco,
E 'l aer nostro, a la mia mente imbruna."
("When the sun bathes in the sea his golden orb,
And darkens our atmosphere and my mind.")
But Gray has given a grotesque turn to his original.

6 One of Gray's favourite inversions.

7 Cf. *Macbeth*, act iii. scene 2—
"The shard-borne beetle, with his drowsy hums,
Hath rung night's yawning peal."
Notice the different sentiments which the same natural object evokes in different moods.

10 The 'ignavus bubo' of Ovid. Cf.
"The wailing owl
Screams solitary to the mournful moon."
[Point out a blot in this line.] *Mallett.*
11 *Bower.* Properly 'chamber.'
13 "Or against the rugged bark of some broad elm."
MILTON, *Comus.*
17 Milton, *Paradise Lost*, ix. 192—
"Now when, as sacred light began to dawn
In Eden on the humid flowers, that breathed
Their morning incense."
18 Tennyson, *Princess*—
"The earliest pipe of half-awakened birds."
Vergil, *Æn.*, viii. 455—
"Evandrum ex humili tecto lux suscitat alma,
Et matutini volucrum sub culmine cantus."
19 Milton, *Paradise Lost*, vii. 443—
"The crested cock, whose clarion sounds
The silent hours."
20 [*Lowly bed.* Point out any ambiguity in this expression.].
21 *Lucretius*, iii. 894—
"Jam jam non domus accipiet te laeta, neque uxor
Optima, nec dulces occurrent oscula nati
Praeripere."
22 *Care.* 'Pensum,' 'task.' The phrase is hardly English, and necessitated by the rhyme.
26 Vergil, *Georgics*, i. 94—
"Rastris glebas qui frangit inertes."
27 [*Afield.* What does the *a-* represent?]
28 *Sturdy.* French 'étourdi.' Defined in *Promptorium Parvulorum* as 'unbuxum' ('unyielding'), 'rebellis, contumax,' and so used by Chaucer, Gower, &c.
33 *Heraldry.* Juvenal's 'Stemmata quid faciunt?'
35 *Awaits.* Has by the common consent of editors been altered to 'await,' but 'awaits' is the reading both of Gray's manuscript and of the Editio princeps of 1768. Is not 'the inevitable hour' the subject? Such an inversion is so common with Gray as almost to amount to a mannerism. This too gives a more natural sense to 'awaits.'
37 *You, ye.* Properly 'ye' is nominative, 'you' accusative, and this distinction is observed in our English Bible, though generally disregarded by the Elizabethans, the choice being determined mostly by euphony. Cf. Rowe: "Were you, ye fair, but cautious whom ye trust."
38 [*Trophies.* What is the original meaning?]

Clio the muse of History
Euterpe   "   "   " Lyric poetry
Thalia   "   "   " Comedy
Melpomene "   "   " Tragedy
Terpsichore "   "   " Coral dance
Polymnia   "   "   " Sublime hymn
Urania   "   "   " Astronomy
Calliope   "   "   " Epic Poetry
Erato   "   "   " Amatory poetry

Feet in a line
x stands for unaccented syllable
u   "   "   accented syllable

(xa) Iambus | (xux) Amphibrach
(ax) Trochee | (xxa) Anapest
(aa) Spondee |
(xx) Pyrrhic |
(axx) Dactyl |

(χa) in a line — name
$(\chi a) \times 2$ — Iambic Mo-nom. / Mononomete
$(\chi a) \times 3$ — Iambic Dimeter
$(\chi a) \times 4$ — Iambic Trimeter
$(\chi a) \times 5$ — Iambic Tetrameter
$(\chi a) \times 6$ — Iambic Pentameter
$(\chi a) \times 7$ — Iambic Hexameter
$(\chi a) \times 7$ — Iambic Heptameter

The same rule applies for the Trochees & Spondees. and so on
___

A verse is a ~~a~~ line of Poetry
A Stanza is a combination of several lines constituting the regular division of a poem
A Foot or measure is a group of syllables taken togethe
A Distich or couplet consists of

NOTES—ELEGY.

39 *Fretted.* The word 'fret' represents at least three distinct forms which have been assimilated; but it is difficult to disentangle the different meanings, and assign each to its original. 1. The Old English 'freten,' 'to eat;' cf. German 'fressen' (for 'ver-essen'), 'a moth fretting a garment.' [What other meaning belongs to this head?] 2. There is another Old English word (probably connected with the first) 'fraet,' 'fraetwan,' 'ornament,' 'to ornament.' 3. 'Fret' in architecture and heraldry is from a Roman root; Italian 'ferrata," French 'fretté,' properly iron grating or trellis-work; so of the lozenge-shaped bars crossing one another in a coat of arms, or the cross bands of a ceiling; Latin 'laquearia.' 4. 'Frets,' the stops or keys of a musical instrument, is of uncertain origin. [Class under three heads, and explain, the following quotations from Shakespeare: "This majestical roof, fretted with golden fire." "Though you can fret me, yet you cannot play upon me." "Yon grey lines that fret the clouds." "His fretted fortunes gave him hope and fear." "He's fretted like a gummed velvet." "The roof of the chamber with golden cherubims is fretted."

40 *Anthem.* 'Anthem' and 'antiphon' are doublets. Old English 'antefne,' as we find it in the *Ancren Riwle* (1220). [How did this class of words come into English?]

41 *Storied urn.* Cf. *Il Penseroso*, 159, "storied windows." The epithet is not happily transferred, as the monumental urn (a survival of the cinerary urn of the Romans) has no story inscribed on it.

Animated. Cf. Pope's—
  "Lely on animated canvas stole
    The sleepy eye, that spoke the languid soul."
And Vergil's 'spirantia aera,' and 'viros de marmore voltus.'

47 Tickell has "Proud names that once the reins of empire held;" and Gray first wrote 'reins.' [Can you suggest a reason for the emendation?]

50 [*Unroll.* Justify the metaphor.]

51 *Rage.* Constantly used by Pope and his school as a synonym of poetic inspiration, genius.

53 *Many a.* A difficult idiom. We find it as early as Layamon's *Brut* (*circ.* 1205), where it is declined as a single word—"Unimete folc monianes cunnes" (immense folk of many a kin). This is sufficient to disprove Trench's conjecture that 'many' represents the French 'mesnie;' and Barnes's that 'a' represents 'on.' Compare the German 'manch ein.'

52-56 Much learning has been expended in tracing the original of these celebrated lines. Instead of quoting the many parallels more or less close, it will be more profitable to give the wise remarks of Lowell on imitations in general, from his essay on Dryden : " He certainly gave even a liberal interpretation to Molière's rule of taking his own property when he found it, though he sometimes blundered awkwardly about what was properly *his;* but in literature it should be remembered *a thing always becomes his at last who says it best, and that makes it his own.* . . . For example, Waller calls the Duke of York's flag

"'His dreadful streamer, like a comet's hair.'

And this, I believe, is the first application of the celestial portent to this particular comparison. Yet Milton's 'imperial ensign' waves defiant behind his impregnable lines ; and even Campbell flaunts his 'meteor flag' in Waller's face. Gray's *Bard* might be sent to the lock-up, but even he would find bail.

' C'est imiter quelqu'un que de planter des choux.'"

57 Gray wisely substituted Hampden and Cromwell for Brutus and Julius of the first draft.

Hampden refused the payment of ship-money in 1637.—See Bright, ii. 630.

[What should you gather from this stanza as to Gray's political opinions? Is he Cavalier or Roundhead, Tory or Whig?]

61-64 [Illustrate by examples each line.]

63 From Tickell—

"To scatter blessings o'er the British land."

65 ['He forbad to go' is not English. Can you justify the construction here?]

68 From Shakespeare, *Henry V.*, act iii. scene 3—

"The *gates of mercy* shall be all shut up."

69 *Conscious truth.* The truth of which they are conscious, which they know, and fain would testify.

71 The age of Queen Anne was the age of patronage and fulsome dedication.—See Macaulay's *Essay on Boswell's Life of Johnson.* Thus Pope is constantly boasting that he is a unique exception to the prevailing vice, and satirizing men like Bufo (Halifax),

" I ed with soft dedication all day long."

73 From Drummond, *Sonnet* 49—

" Far from the madding worldling's hoarse discords."

Shakespeare has "madding Dido," and Milton "madding wheels." The construction is, 'The wishes of them who were far,' &c.

77 *Yet.* "Humble as they are, and wanting stately tombs."

78 *Still.* 'Notwithstanding'; but the position of the word is awkward.

[79 *Deck'd.* 'Protect.' Is this a just rhyme?]

Rhimes. So spelt by Gray. 'Rime' is correct (Old English for number). 'Rhyme' is due to the false derivation from Greek $\rho\upsilon\theta\mu\delta s$.

heterogeneous couplets, four measures
with pairs of rhymes
Octavii Triplets, four measures with
rhymes regularly in successions
Heroic couplets four measures with
pairs of rhymes.
Heroic Triplets four measures with

Ballad stanza: — consists of $4(8ca)\times 4$. The 1st line consists of $4(8ca)\times 3$. The 2nd line consists of $2\frac{nd}{4}$. The 3rd and 4th are like 1st and 2nd. The lines consist of $(8ca)4$ common Metre. The 1st line consists of $4(8ca)3$. The 2nd line consists of $4(8ca)$ — the 2 stanza consists of 4 lines which rhyme alternately. The 4 lines which comporte rhyme alternately. The 4 lines 3 which Long metre: The 4 lines of equal length. Each stanza has 4 equal lengths. The lines rhyme alternately consisting of $4(8ca)$. The lines rhyme in times alternately and sometimes in

NOTES—ELEGY.

81 *Muse.* 'Poet.' So in Spenser, Shakespeare, Milton, Dryden, &c. Cf. Shakespeare, *Sonnet* 21—
"So is it not with me as with that muse,
Stirred by a painted beauty to his verse."
84 *That teach.* Strict grammar would require the singular.
Moralist. Used loosely for one who learns or practices morals.
85 It is a moot point, which it is impossible to determine, whether *to dumb forgetfulness a prey* is in apposition to 'who,' or to 'being.' The first interpretation is the simplest in construction; the second, in meaning. In the first case the question is really contained in the appositional clause, 'Who being a prey to forgetfulness resigned life' = 'Who in resigning life ever thought he would be forgotten.' In the second case the meaning will be, 'Who ever resigned this life to oblivion,' = 'Who ever was content to die and be forgotten.'
86 Cf. *Adriani morientis ad animam*—
"Animula vagula blandula.
Hospes, comesque corporis,
Quae nunc abibis in loca?
Pallidula, rigida, nudula,
Nec, ut soles, dabis joca."
87 Cf. Lucretius, "luminis oras."
89 Compare the 'uncouth rhimes' of Drayton—
"It is some comfort to a wretch to die
(If there be comfort in the way of death),
To have some friend or kind alliance by,
To be officious at the parting breath."
90 *Pious drops.* The 'piae lacrimae' of Ovid. 'Tears of affection.'
92 Chaucer, *Reve's Prologue*, 3880, has
"Yet in oure aisshen cold is fyr yreken (raked)."
The similarity is in the words, not the sense. The Reve says that even in old age the passions of youth are warm. Gray means even after death the yearning for affection still lives.
Gray himself quotes Petrarch, *Sonnets*—
"Ch' i veggio nel pensier, dolce mio fuoco,
Fredda una lingua e due begli occhi chiusi,
Rimaner doppo noi pien di faville."
93 *For thee.* 'As for thee.'
95 *Chance.* Cf. adverbial use of 'fors.'
96 *Kindred spirit.* One like the poet, 'mindful of the unhonour'd dead.'
97 *Swain.* First meaning, 'a boy;' then 'a servant;' lastly, in pastoral poetry, used for 'a lover.'

98 Cf. *Comus*, 138—
"Ere the babbling eastern scout,
The nice morn, on the Indian steep
From his cabined loophole peep."

100 *Upland*. Milton (*L'Allegro*, 92) uses 'upland' in the older sense of 'country;' but Gray is thinking rather of another passage of Milton (*Lycidas*, 25)—
"Ere the high lawns appeared
Under the opening eyelids of the morn."

102 *As You Like It*, act ii. scene 1—
"He lay along
Under an oak, whose antique root peep'd out
Upon the brook that brawls along the wood."

104 Cf. Burns, *Epistle to William Simpson*—
"The muse, nae Poet ever fand her,
Till by himsel' he learn'd to wander
Adown some trotting burn's meander,
An' no think lang;
O sweet, to stray an' pensive ponder
A heart-felt sang!"

105 From closeness of texture we get the idea of proximity.

106 *Wayward*. Old English 'waeward,' and so probably connected with 'woe,' not 'way.' The analogies of 'froward,' 'toward,' may, however, have influenced the meaning.

107 "Low spirits are my true and faithful companions; they get up with me, go to bed with me, make journeys and returns as I do; nay, and pay visits, and will even affect to be jocose, and force a feeble laugh with me; but most commonly we sit alone together, and are the prettiest insipid company in the world." GRAY to West, August, 1737. See Macaulay's somewhat brutal remarks in *Essay on Moore's Life of Byron*, ad fin.: "To people who are unacquainted with real calamity, 'nothing is so dainty sweet as lovely melancholy.' This faint image of sorrow has in all ages been considered as an agreeable excitement. Old gentlemen and middle-aged gentlemen have so many real causes of sadness that they are rarely inclined 'to be as sad as night only for wantonness.' Indeed, they want the power almost as much as the inclination. We know very few persons engaged in active life who, even if they were to procure stools to be melancholy upon, and were to sit down with all the premeditation of Master Stephen, would be able to enjoy much of what somebody calls the 'ecstasy of woe.'"

114 *Church-way path*. The phrase occurs in *Midsummer Night's Dream*, act v., sc. 1, l. 386. There is no need to suppose a corruption of 'hay' ('enclosure'), or to correct 'churchyard.'

Hallelujah Mater:— The stamps
of eight sizes, the first 4 considered
the last 4 considered (o.a.) 4
Besides these there are considered
of Jourdrie, Fuchsie and Anapes
measures. Each kind can be eas-
ascertained by the description
given.

*Dramatic + Poetry...intituled (to be acted
Pastoral Represent Shepherd Life;
Satirical: Poetry to improve
Didactic* Poetry intended to instruct us
Elegise Poetry treats of solemn + Mour
  subjects.
  several pause, a pause arch et cute
  verse into two pause
  Punctuation pauses
  found at end of l---

NOTES—ELEGY.

115 *Lay.* Used, *metri gratia*, for 'verse.' 'Lay' is probably a Celtic word, and means properly 'a ballad, or song recited to music.'

Before the *Epitaph* Gray originally inserted this stanza—

"There scattered oft, the earliest of the year,
  By hands unseen, are showers of violets found;
The redbreast loves to build and warble there,
  And little footsteps lightly print the ground."

Gray afterwards omitted the lines, as forming too long a parenthesis; but they are in themselves as exquisite as anything he ever wrote.

119 Cf. Horace, *Odes*, iv. 3, 1—

"Quem tu Melpomene semel
 Nascentem placido lumine videris."

[In what sense did *science* smile on Gray's birth?]

124 *A friend.* An editor annotates: "The friend whom Gray gained from heaven was Mason." Correct him.

[How far is the *Epitaph* true to Gray's character, as you know it from his life?]

15- Stereup
2

MR. GRAY TO MR. WALPOLE.

ASH-WEDNESDAY, CAMBRIDGE, 1751.

MY DEAR SIR,—You have indeed conducted with great decency my little *misfortune:* you have taken a paternal care of it, and expressed much more kindness than could have been expressed from so near a relation. But we are all frail; and I hope to do as much for you another time.

Nurse Dodsley has given it a pinch or two in the cradle, that (I doubt) it will bear the marks of as long as it lives. But no matter: we have ourselves suffered under her hands before now; and besides, it will only look the more careless and by *accident* as it were. I thank you for your advertisement, which saves my honour, and in a manner *bien flatteuse pour moi*, who should be put to it even to make myself a compliment in good English.

You will take me for a mere poet, and a fetcher and carrier of sing-song, if I tell you that I intend to send you the beginning of a drama,* not mine, thank God, as you will believe, when you hear it is finished, but wrote by a person whom I have a very good opinion of. It is (unfortunately) in the manner of the ancient drama, with choruses, which I am to my shame the occasion of; for, as great part of it was at first written in that form, I would not suffer him to change it to a play fit for the stage, and as he intended, because the lyric parts are the best of it, they must have been lost. The story is Saxon, and the language has a tang of Shakespeare, that suits an old-fashioned fable very well. In short I don't do it merely to amuse you, but for the sake of the author, who wants a judge, and so I would lend him *mine:* yet not without your leave, lest you should have us up to dirty our stockings at the bar of your house, for wasting the time and politics of the *nation.* Adieu, Sir!—I am, ever yours, T. GRAY.

---

* This was the *Elfrida* of Mr. Mason.

TO AVOID CONFUSION, ASK FOR

MILLER'S SWINTON'S LANGUAGE LESSONS,

The new Authorized Grammar,

MILLER'S SWINTON'S LANGUAGE LESSONS,

BY J. A. McMILLAN, B. A.

The only Edition prepared as an Introductory Text Book to Mason's Grammar.

In Miller's Edition of Language Lessons **The Definitions of the Parts of Speech are now made identical with Mason's Grammar.**

The Classification of Pronouns, Verbs, Moods, and General Treatment are the same as in **Mason's Text Book.**

Miller's Edition is prepared as an introductory Text Book for Mason's Grammar, the authorized book for advanced classes for Public Schools, so that what is learned by a pupil in an elementary text-book will not have to be unlearned when the advanced book is used, a serious fault with many of the graded Public School Books.

Miller's Edition contains all the recent examination Papers set for admission to High Schools.

MILLER'S SWINTON'S LANGUAGE LESSONS
is authorised by the Education Department of Ontario,
is adopted by the Schools of Montreal,
is authorised by the Council of Public Instruction, Manitoba.

To the President and Members of the County of Elgin Teachers Association:

In accordance with a motion passed at the last regular meeting of the Association, appointing the undersigned a Committee to consider the respective merits of different English Grammars, with a view to suggest the most suitable one for Public Schools, we beg leave to report, that, after fully comparing the various editions that have been recommended, we believe that "Miller's Swinton's Language Lessons" is best adapted to the wants of junior pupils and would urge its authorization on the Government, and its introduction into our Public Schools.

St. Thomas, Nov. 30th, 1878.

A. F. BUTLER, Co. Inspector.
J. McLEAN, Town Inspector.
J. MILLER, M.A., Head Master St. Thomas High School.
A. STEELE, B.A., " Aylmer High School.
N. M. CAMPBELL, " Co. of Elgin Model School.

It was moved and seconded that the report be received and adopted.—Carried unanimously.

Price, Cloth Extra, - 25c.

ADAM MILLER & CO.

The New. Authorized Elementary Grammar.

MILLER'S SWINTON'S LANGUAGE LESSONS.

MILLER's Swinton's Language Lessons is used exclusively in nearly all the Principal Public and Model Schools of Ontario. Among them are

Ottawa,	Hamilton,	Whitby, Port Hope, Coboarg, Mitchell,
Napanee,	Brockville,	Lindsay,	St. Catharines,
Strathroy,	Meaford,	Uxbridge,	Brantford,
Windsor,	Clinton,	St. Thomas,	Perth,
Seaforth,	Listowel,	Bracebridge,	Belleville.

Adopted by the Protestant Schools of Montreal and Levi College, Quebec, Schools of Winnipeg, Manitoba, and St. John's, New Foundland.

Resolution passed unanimously by the Teachers' Association, (North Huron), held at Brussels, May 17, 1878 " Resolved, That the Teachers at this Convention are of opinion that ' MILLER's Swinton Language Lessons,' by McMillan, is the best introductory work on Grammar for Public School use, since the definitions, classification and general treatment are extremely simple and satisfactory." \

In my opinion the best introductory Text-book to Mason's Grammar. All pupils who intend to enter a High School or to become students for Teachers' Certificates, would save time by using it.

W. J. CARSON, H. M.,
Model School, London.

The definition's in " Miller's Swinton Language Lessons" are brief, clear and exact, and leave little to be unlearned in after years. The arrangement of the subjects is logical and progressive, and the book admirably helps the judicious teacher in making correct thinkers and ready readers and writers.

B. W. WOOD,
1st.*A Provincial H., P. S., Trenton Falls*

Be careful to ask for MILLER'S SWINTON, as other editions are in the market.

ENGLISH GRAMMAR
BY C. P. MASON, B.A., F.C.P.,
FELLOW OF UNIVERSITY COLLEGE, LONDON,

With Examination Papers by W. HOUSTON, M.A.

PRICE 75 CENTS.

ALEX. SIM, M.A., H. M., H. S., Oakville
Upwards of three years ago I asked a grammar school nspector in the old country to send me the best grammar publi hed there. He immediately sent me Mason.

A. P. KNIGHT, M.A., H.M., Kingston Collegiate Institute.
Incomparably the best text book for the senior classes of our high schools that has yet been offered to the Canadian public.

J. KING, M.A., L.L.D., Principal, Caledonia, H. S.
Mason's grammar will be found a most valuable class-book especially for the instruction of advanced classes in English. The chapter on the Analysis of difficult sentences is of itself sufficient to place the work far beyond any English grammar hitherto before the Canadian public.

RICHARD LEWIS, H. M., Dufferin School Toronto.
As a philosophical treatise its discussion of doubtful points and its excellent methods and definitions cannot fail to give it a high rank in the estimation of the best judges of such works—the school teachers of the country. It has reached a twenty-first edition in England and I have no doubt it will meet with the same high appreciation in this Province.

JOHN SHAW, H. M., H. S., Omemee.
* * * Mason's Grammar is just such a book as many teachers have been hoping to see introduced into our schools, its method being to teach the subject by explanation, definition and abundant illustrations without stereotyped rules thereby making the study even attractive.

D. C. MacHENRY, B. A., H. M., Cobourg Col. Institute.
It is an excellent and reliable work. It will be well received by teachers and advanced pupils.

JOHN JOHNSTON, P. S. I., Belleville and South Hastings.
Of all the grammars that I have seen, I consider Mason's the best.

J. MORRISON, M.A., M.D., Head Master, High School, Newmarket.
I have ordered it to be used in this school. I consider it by far the best English grammar for high school purposes that has yet appeared. With "Mason" and "Fleming" nothing more seems to be desired.

THE EPOCH PRIMER
OF ENGLISH HISTORY.

Being an Introductory Volume to the series of *Epochs of English History*, by the Rev. MANDELL CREIGHTON, M. A., late Fellow and Tutor of Merton College, Oxford; Editor of 'Epochs of English History.' Fcp. 8vo. pp 148, price 30 cts. cloth.

'In making history attractive to the young the Author has proved his aptitude in a department of literature in which few distinguish themselves..... The narrative is so sustained that those who take it up will have a desire to read it to the end.'
DUNDEE ADVERTISER.

'This volume is intended to be introductory to the *Epochs of English History*, and nothing could be better adapted for that purpose. The little book is admirably done in all respects, and ought to have the effect of sending pupils to other and fuller sources of historical knowledge.' SCOTSMAN.

'Mr CREIGHTON'S introduction to the *Epochs of English History* covers in a hundred and forty pages more than 1800 years, but having regard to its extreme condensation is well worthy of notice. On the whole the work is admirably done, and it will no doubt obtain a very considerable sale.'
ATHENÆUM.

'An admirable little book that can scarcely fail to obtain a considerable popularity, notwithstanding the great number of previous attempts made to relate the history of England in a very small compass.....In this epitome the epochs become chapters, but an interesting account is given of such events as are likely to be attractive, or even moderately intelligible to young readers.' WELSHMAN.

'The excellent series of little books published under the title of *Epochs of English History*, edited by the Rev. MANDELL CREIGHTON, M. A., and written by various able and eminent writers being now complete, the Editor has prepared an introductory volume, called the *Epoch Primer*, comprising a concise summary of the whole series. The special value of this historical outline is that it gives the reader a comprehensive view of the course of memorable events and epochs and enables him to see how they have each contributed to make the British Nation what it is at the present day.'
LITERARY WORLD.

'As all the leading features—political, social and popular—are given with much impartiality, it can hardly fail to become a school class-book of great utility.' WORCESTER JOURNAL.

'The Rev. MANDELL CREIGHTON has really succeeded in making an admirable resume of the whole of the principle events in English history, from the time of the Roman Invasion down to the passing of the Irish Land Act in 1870. Interesting, intelligible and clear, it will prove of great value in the elementary schools of the kingdom; and those advanced in years might find it very handy and useful for casual reference.' NORTHAMPTON HERALD.

'This volume, taken with the eight small volumes containing the accounts of the different epochs, presents what may be regarded as the most thorough course of elementary English History ever published........Well suited for middle class schools, this series may also be studied with advantage by senior students, who will find, instead of the mass of apparently unconnected facts which is too often presented in such works, a careful tracing-out of the real current of history, and an intelligible account of the progress of the nation and its institutions.'
ABERDEEN JOURNAL.

'The whole series may be safely commended to the notice of parents and teachers anxious to find a suitable work on English history for their children, inasmuch as the several volumes are simply and intelligibly written, without being overloaded with details, and care has been taken to bring every subject treated on within the comprehension of the young. The namby-pamby element, which is so often conspicuous in histories for children is entirely absent, and the works in question are certainly amongst the best of the kind yet issued. The little volume now under notice, which brings the series to a close, is fully equal in every respect to the preceding ones, and it will be found exceedingly useful to every one who may have to teach English history.'
LEAMINGTON COURIER.

CREIGHTON'S EPOCHS OF ENGLISH HISTORY

Rev. GEO. BLAIR, M.A., I. P. S., Grenville County.

"This little work, published in eight miniature volumes, at 20c. each, is peculiarly adapted for use in our Public and High Schools. Presented in this simple and attractive form, each of the great epochs of English History can be cheaply, easily, and thoroughly mastered before proceeding to the next."

THOS. CARSCADDEN, B.A., Head Master, High School, Richmond Hill.

"I can most cordially recommend them to all students who are candidates for the Intermediate, or teachers' examinations."

J. TURNBULL, B.A., Principal High School, Clinton.

"I have examined the 'Epochs of English History' and have formed a very high opinion of them, so much so, that I intend to introduce them into the High School here. As to the size and expense they have hit the happy mean, containing all that is really necessary and nothing more."

H. J. GIBSON, B.A., Head Master, Renfrew, H. School.

"I have carefully examined your 'Epochs of History,' and believe them to be admirably adapted for preparing teachers for certificates. They are very neatly got up."

JOHN E. BRYANT, B.A., Clinton.

"I have been anxiously waiting for a Canadian edition of these delightful little books, and now that we have these, I shall introduce them into my classes as soon as possible."

A. DINGWALL FORDYCE, P. S. I., Fergus.

"I think it is a great mistake, at a time when imagination is peculiarly vivid, to expect history to be studied from the *bare bones* laid down, and that the little work referred to has been prepared in a simple, interesting way for those commencing the study of history, and fitted to carry them on by the grasp they can take of the subject as it is presented, and as one event is connected with another, I think some such introductory work was much needed."

J. M. PLATT, M.D., P. S. I., Picton.

"Neatness of 'get up;' simplicity of language; faithfulness of record; perfection in arrangement; interest of narrative; conciseness and freedom from dryness; or recital of facts, are but a few of the recommendations of these beautiful little works."

F. H. MICHEL, B.A., H. M., H. S., Perth.

"It has been said that a book that would supply the place of 'Collier's British History' could not be obtained. This is more than answered by the 'Epochs of English History.' They proceed on the basis on which history should be taught. Divisions are made according to the inception and cessation of those forces that brought about changes in the English Constitution, while principles are clearly communicated and systematized. Not beyond the capabilities of younger children, they are also adapted for use in higher classes."

ROBT. RODGERS, Inspector of Public Schools, Collingwood.

"As an aid to the teacher they are invaluable."

GUELPH MERCURY.

"The style is simple, and adapted to the capacity of children at school."

Mental Arithmetic.

By J. A. McLELLAN, M.A., LL.D., *Inspector of High Schools, Ont.*

PART 1.—FUNDAMENTAL RULES, FRACTIONS, ANALYSIS. PRICE, 30c.

PART II.—PERCENTAGE, RATIO, PROPORTION, &C. PRICE, 45C.

W. D. DIMOCK, A.B., H.M.
Provincial Model School, Nova Scotia.

Dr. McLellan's Mental Arithmetic supplies a want that we should have had supplied in our Schools long ago. Same progress cannot be made in Mathematical work, unless what we call Mental Arithmetic is thoroughly and systematically pursued. A boy who is conversant with the principles of Mental Arithmetic, as given in this little text-book, is worth as a clerk or accountant 50 per cent more than the prodigy who can boast of having "gone" through his written arithmetic half a dozen times.

J. S. DEACON, Principal Ingersoll Model School.
Dr. McLellan's Mental Arithmetic, Part I., is a credit to Canadians, and it supplies a long-felt want. It is just what is wanted for "waking up mind" in the school room. After two weeks use of the book with my class I am convinced that it is much superior to any of the American texts that have been used here both as to the grading of questions and the style of the problems.

J. A. CLARKE, M.A., H.M.H.S., Picton.
Dr. McLellan's Mental Arithmetic contains a great number of useful problems well adapted to develop by regular gradations the thinking powers of the pupil, and to suggest similar examples for the use of the teacher.

D. J. GOGGIN, Head Master Model and Public Schools, Port Hope.
Simple in its arrangement, varied in its types of practical questions and sugggestive in its methods, it is the best book of its kind that I have examined.

From THE WESLEYAN, Halifax, Nova Scotia.
The series bids fair to take a good place in scholastic work.

EXAMINATION PAPERS
IN
ARITHMETIC;

By J. A. McLELLAN, LL.D., Inspector High Schools, and THOS. KIRKLAND, M.A., Science Master, Normal School, Toronto.

PRICE $1.00.

From the GUELPH MERCURY.

. . . The work is divided into six chapters. The first is on the Unitary Method, and gives solutions showing its application to a variety of problems, in Simple and Compound Proportion; Percentage, Interest, Discount, Profit and Loss; Proportional Parts, Partnership; Chain Rule, Exchange, Alligation; Commission, Insurance. &c., Stocks, and Miscellaneous Problems. The second is on Elementary Rules, Measures and Multiples, Vulgar and Decimal Fractions. The third contains Examination Papers for entrance into High Schools and Collegiate Institutes, the fourth for candidates for third-class certificates, the fifth for candidates for the Intermediate Examination and second-class certificates, and the sixth for candidates for third-class certificates and University Honours. It will be observed that the work begins with the fundamental rules—those principles to be acquired when a pupil first enters upon the study of Arithmetic, and carries him forward till prepared for the highest class of certificates and for Honours of the University. . . . Teachers will find in it a necessary help in supplying questions to give their classes. Those who aspire to be teachers cannot have a better guide—indeed there is not so good a one—on the subject with which it is occupied.

From the ADVERTISER.

. . . By all who are groping after some method better than they have at present, this volume will be cordially welcomed, and many who have never suspected the possibility of accomplishing so much by independent methods, will be, by a perusal of the introductory chapter, impelled to think for themselves, and enabled to teach their pupils how to do so. . . . It is far superior to anything of the kind ever introduced into this country. . . . The typographical appearance of the work is of a very high character—quite equal, in fact, to anything of the kind issued by the best publishing houses of London or New York.

From the TELESCOPE.

. . . The plan of the work is excellent, the exercises being arranged progressively, each series preparing the student for the next. The problems are all original, and so constructed as to prevent the student using any purely mechanical methods of solution. . . . We should really feel proud of our Canadian Authors and publishing houses, when we consider the infancy of our country and the progress it has made and is making in educational matters, and particularly in the recently published educational works.

Highly Commended by the *Press* of Canada and
the United States.

The 4th Edition. 50th Thousand issued within nine months.

Authorized by the Education Department of Prince Edward Island, introduced in many of the principal Public Schools of the Provinces of Ontario and Quebec.

ELEMENTARY ARITHMETIC
ON THE UNITARY METHOD.

By THOMAS KIRKLAND, M.A., Science Master Normal School, Toronto, and WILLIAM SCOTT, B.A., Head Master Model School, Toronto.

Cloth Extra. 176 pages. Price 25 cents.

A. B. WESTERFELT, H.M. Model School, Mt. Forest.

Kirkland & Scott's Elementary Arithmetic is an excellent work. It is intensely practical.

SAML. R. BROWN, Head Teacher, Sep. Schools, London, Ont.

I have carefully examined your Elementary, (by Kirkland & Scott) and I consider it far superior to any other book of the kind with which I am acquainted, and just what we require for our junior classes. I will introduce it immediately.

ST. MARY'S ARGUS.

The arrangement of the work is thoroughly rational, the oral and slate exercises are exactly what is needed, being sufficiently simple and yet well calculated to develop the thinking faculties while the adoption of the simple and uniform system of working all problems by analysis and deduction makes the book correspond with the method of teaching arithmetic now being adopted by all intelligent teachers.

EDUCATIONAL JOURNAL OF VIRGINIA.

This volume presents in a condensed form all that is needed in an elementary book.

JOHN McINTOSH, Principal Granby Academy.

The Elementary Arithmetic, by Kirkland and Scott, is estimated so highly by me, that I shall take immediate steps to have it introduced into the Academy, of which I have charge. As an introductory work, there is no text-book in use which equals it in all that is necessary both from the standpoint of the teacher and pupil.

Miller & Co.'s Educational Series.

HAMBLIN SMITH'S
MATHEMATICAL WORKS,
ARE USED ALMOST EXCLUSIVELY

In the Normal and Model Schools, Toronto; Upper Canada College; Hamilton and Brantford Collegiate Institutes; Bowmanville, Berlin, Belleville, and a large number of leading High Schools in the Province.

HAMBLIN SMITH'S ALGEBRA,

With Appendix, by Alfred Baker, B.A., Mathematical Tutor, University College, Toronto. Price, 90 cents.

THOMAS KIRKLAND, M.A., Science Master, Normal School.

"It is the text-book on Algebra for candidates for second-class certificates, and for the Intermediate Examination. Not the least valuable part of it is the Appendix by Mr. Baker."

GEO. DICKSON, B.A., Head Master, Collegiate Institute, Hamilton.

"Arrangement of subjects good; explanations and proofs exhaustive, concise and clear; examples, for the most part from University and College Examination Papers, are numerous, easy and progressive. There is no better Algebra in use in our High Schools and Collegiate Institutes."

WM. R. RIDDELL, B.A., B.Sc., Mathematical Master, Normal School, Ottawa.

"The Algebra is admirable, and well adapted as a general textbook."

W. E. TILLEY, B.A., Mathematical Master, Bowmanville High School.

"I look on the Algebra as decidedly the best Elementary Work on the subject we have. The examples are excellent and well arranged. The explanations are easily understood.

R. DAWSON, B.A., T.C.D., Head Master, High School, Belleville.

"With Mr. Baker's admirable Appendix, there would seem to be nothing left to be desired. We have now a first-class book, well adapted in all respects to the wants of pupils of all grades, from the beginner in our Public Schools to the most advanced student in our Collegiate Institutes and High Schools. Its publication is a great boon to the over-worked mathematical teachers of the Province

www.ingramcontent.com/pod-product-compliance
Lightning Source LLC
Chambersburg PA
CBHW020253170426
43202CB00008B/353